ALGERNON, CHARLIE, AND I

ALGERNON, CHARLIE, AND I

A Writer's Journey

DANIEL KEYES

A Harvest Book · Harcourt, Inc.

Orlando   Austin   New York   San Diego   Toronto   London

www.HarcourtBooks.com

First published by Challenge Press, 2000

Library of Congress Cataloging-in-Publication Data
Keyes, Daniel.
Algernon, Charlie, and I: a writer's journey/Daniel Keyes.—1st Harvest ed.
p.   cm.—(A Harvest book)
ISBN 0-15-602999-5
1. Keyes, Daniel. Flowers for Algernon—Sources. 2. People with mental
disabilities in literature. 3. People with mental disabilities—Fiction.
4. Gifted persons—Fiction. 5. Brain—Surgery—Fiction. I. Title.
PS3561.E769F56 2004b
813'.54—dc22   2004011445

Text set in AGaramond
Designed by Cathy Riggs

Printed in the United States of America
First Harvest edition 2004

A C E G I K J H F D B

For my wife Aurea,
who tended the dream garden
so "Flowers" *could grow.*

|||||||||||||||||||||||

CONTENTS

PART ONE

||||||||||||||||||||||

The Maze of Time

1

||||||||||||||||||||||

My Writing Cellar

I NEVER THOUGHT it would happen to me.

When I was very young and very nearsighted—20/400 vision, everything blurred without my eyeglasses—I believed that someday I'd go blind. So I planned ahead. I strove to be neat, a place for everything and everything in its place. I blindfolded myself and practiced retrieving things without seeing, and I was proud that I could find anything quickly in the dark.

I didn't go blind. In fact, with eyeglasses my vision is excellent.

I can still put my hands on most things I possess. Not because I remember where I put them, but because I take the time to put them away carefully, in logical places. I just have to remember where they belong. What's happening to me is something I never considered. I start out to do something, go somewhere, walk into another room to get something, but then I have to pause. What am I looking for? Then it quickly clicks into place. It's momentary but frightening. And I think of Charlie Gordon at the end of *Flowers for Algernon*, saying, *"I remember I did something but I don't remember what."*

Why am I thinking of the fictional character I created more than forty years ago? I try to put him out of my mind, but he won't let me.

Charlie is haunting me, and I've got to find out why.

I've decided the only way I can put him to rest is to go back through the maze of time, search for his origins, and exorcise the ghosts of memories past. Perhaps, along the way, I'll also learn when, how, and why I became a writer.

Getting started is the hardest thing. I tell myself, you've got the material. You don't have to make it up—just remember it, shape it. And you don't have to create a fictional narrator's voice the way you did for the story and then the novel. This is you, writing about writing, and remembering the secrets of your own life that became the life of Charlie Gordon.

The opening of the story echoes in my mind: *"Dr. Strauss says I shud rite down what I think and evrey thing that happins to me from now on. I dont know why but he says its importint so they will see if they will use me. I hope they use me. Miss Kinnian says maybe they can make me smart. I want to be smart. My name is Charlie Gordon..."*

Although the original novelette begins with those words, that's not how it all started. Nor are his final words about putting *"flowrs... in the bak yard"* the end of his story. I remember clearly where I was the day the ideas that sparked the story first occurred to me.

One crisp April morning in 1945, I climbed the steps to the elevated platform of the Sutter Avenue BMT station in Brownsville, Brooklyn. I'd have a ten- or fifteen-minute wait for the train that would take me to Manhattan, where I would change for the local to the Washington Square branch of New York University.

I recall wondering where I would get the money for the fall semester. My freshman year had used up most of the savings I'd accumulated by working at several jobs, but there wouldn't be enough left to pay for three more years at NYU.

As I took the nickel fare out of my pocket and glanced at it, I remembered my father Willie once admitting to me that when he had been looking for work during the Great Depression, he would walk the ten miles from our two-room apartment, through Brooklyn, and across the Manhattan Bridge each morning and back home each night to save two nickels.

Often, Dad would leave while it was still dark before I awoke, but sometimes I would be up early enough to catch a glimpse of him at the kitchen table, dipping a roll into his coffee. That was his breakfast. For me there was always hot cereal, and sometimes an egg.

Watching him stare into space, I assumed his mind was blank. Now, I realize he was trying to figure out ways to pay our debts. Then he would get up from the table, pat me on the head, tell me to be good in school and study hard. Back then, I thought he was going to his job. I didn't learn until much later that he was ashamed of being out of work.

Maybe this nickel in my hand was one of those he saved.

I dropped it into the slot and pushed through the turnstile. Someday, perhaps I'd retrace his footsteps, walking from Brownsville to Manhattan, to know what it had been like for him. I thought about it, but I never did it.

I think of experiences and images like these as being stored in the *root cellar* of my mind, hibernating in the dark until they are ready for stories.

Most writers have their own metaphors for stored-away scraps and memories. William Faulkner called his writing place a *workshop* and referred to his mental storage place as a *lumber room,* to which he'd go when he needed odds and ends for the fiction he was building.

My mental storage place was in a part of our landlord's cellar, near the coal bin, in the space under the stairs which he allowed my parents to use for storage. Once, when I was big enough to climb down the cellar stairs, I discovered that's where my parents hid my old toys.

I see my brown teddy bear and stuffed giraffe, and Tinkertoy, and Erector set, and tricycle, and roller skates and childhood books—some of them coloring books with line drawings still to fill in with crayons. For me it solved a mystery of toys that vanished when I'd grown tired of them, and others that reappeared in their place.

Even now, I can smell the dank air and the odor of coal in the nearby bin beside the furnace. I see the steel shaft from the coal truck inserted through the cellar window and then, almost immediately, I hear coal clattering down the slide into the coal bin. Our landlord, Mr. Pincus, opens the cast-iron door of the furnace, and stokes it with a poker. I smell wet coal as he shovels it in, and feel heat from the blaze.

Somewhere between the coal bin and the furnace—in the root cellar of my mind—ideas, images, scenes, and dreams wait in the dark until I need them.

Remembering my childhood toy hiding place, as I waited for the train, I thought of my mother and father. I mused over the coincidence that both of their parents—unknown to each other—had made their way across Europe to Canada to New York City. There, Betty and Willie met for the first time. They soon married and had me, their first child, in 1927: the year Lindbergh flew nonstop from New York to Paris, and Al Jolson played the Jazz Singer in the first talking movie.

During those years of hope and excess that later became known as the Jazz Age, my parents, like many other new Americans, went to parties, and danced the Charleston at speakeasies where they could be served illegal gin.

I often wonder what happened to the sepia photograph of my mother, with her bobbed hair and sad dark eyes. I loved to hear her sing popular songs from two-cent lyric sheets and, sometimes, I would sing along with her, our favorite, "Smoke Gets in Your Eyes."

As a boy, in Quebec, Willie had worked for trappers, and learned to speak English, French, Russian, and enough Canadian Indian phrases to trade furs. Although he and my mother had little formal schooling, it became clear to me early in childhood that they respected education, and demanded that I excel in school.

Yet, in my adolescence, I discovered the more I read and learned, the less I could communicate with them. I was losing them—drifting away into my world of books and stories.

Ever since I was a child, they had decided I would become a doctor. When I asked why, my father answered, "Because a doctor is like God. He cures people and saves lives."

My mother added, "When you were a baby, you had an infected mastoid and double pneumonia. A wonderful doctor saved your life."

My father said, "We want you to cure people and save lives."

I accepted their reasons and their obligation. I would work hard, take part-time jobs to earn money, and go to college and medical school. I would become a doctor. Since I loved my parents, I buried my dream of becoming a writer. I declared premed as my major.

Secretly, I wondered if I could become both doctor and writer. I'd read that Somerset Maugham had been educated as a physician and went to sea as a ship's doctor. Chekhov had studied medicine and published his early stories and sketches in journals and papers under the pen name "The Doctor Without Patients." Conan Doyle, unable to support himself as an eye specialist, used his empty consulting room during visiting hours to write the stories of Sherlock Holmes.

An Englishman, a Russian, and a Scotsman had started as physicians and then crossed over into the writing life. By following in their footsteps, perhaps I would be able to fulfill my parents' dream as well as my own.

Almost immediately, I saw the flaw in my solution. Before they became successful authors, all three had failed as doctors.

The crowded train pulled into the station, and I got on, not bothering to look for a seat. It was rush hour, and I would have to stand during the half-hour trip to Union Square. I reached through the crush of work-bound commuters for the white enamel pole in the center of the aisle to steady myself in the lurching train. Most people stared up to avoid eye contact. Feeling depressed, I did the same.

My first year at NYU was nearing an end, and I thought: *My education is driving a wedge between me and the people I love.* And then I wondered: *What would happen if it were possible to increase a person's intelligence?*

That morning, as the train clackety-clacked through the tunnel to Manhattan, I stored away those two ideas: *education could force a wedge between people,* and the storyteller's *"What would happen if...?"*

Later that day, the white mouse happened.

2

||||||||||||||||||||||||||

THE WHITE MOUSE

THE TRAIN PULLED INTO the Eighth Street station, a short walk from Broadway to the Washington Square branch of New York University.

I stopped at a doughnut and coffee shop across from the entrance to the Main Building, and saw a friend at the counter. He waved me to an empty stool beside him. We had been at Thomas Jefferson High School in Brooklyn together but had little to do with each other. He was over six feet tall. I was five-feet-five.

It was only after we discovered we were both premed and found each other in the same biology course at NYU that we became friends. We studied together, testing each other to prepare for exams. Because of the difference in our height, people who saw us called us "Mutt and Jeff" like the characters in a comic strip popular at the time. I called him "Stretch."

I was dunking my doughnut when Stretch said, "Hey, you see the notice? If you volunteer for the military you get exempt from finals."

"You're kidding."

"In Friday's paper," he said. "Any student signing up for duty at least three months before he turns eighteen can enter the service of his choice. After that, it's the Infantry. I'm gonna join the Navy."

"I'll be eighteen on August 9th," I said, "just three months from now. But with my bad eyes, I don't think the Army will draft me."

"You want to take the chance? Lots of guys have been killed. They'll take anyone who breathes."

We paid our checks and headed across the street to the main entrance of NYU.

I knew Stretch would be accepted into the Navy, and I envied him. I loved the sea, or at least the idea of the seafaring life. At sixteen, during my last year in high school, I'd joined the Sea Scouts of America. Our scout ship, the S. S. S. *Flying Dutchman III*, was an old liberty boat converted into a cabin cruiser. During the spring break, we scraped and primed and painted her hull, and the following summer we cruised up and down the East River.

At meetings during which new sea scouts were sworn in, the captain would tell the story of the legendary vessel after whom we were named. The S. S. S. *Flying Dutchman* had carried a cargo of gold, and there had been a brutal murder aboard. After that, a plague broke out among the crew, and no port would allow the ship to enter. According to seamen's stories, the spectral ship still drifts sea-tossed, its men never to return home. It is said that, to this day, the ship can be seen in stormy weather off the Cape of Good Hope, an eternal omen of bad luck.

The captain embellished the story each time he told it, and I'd become curious and looked it up on my own. What he didn't tell us were some of the other legends, like the one that says the curse can be lifted if the captain finds a woman willing to sacrifice everything for his sake.

I told that version to some of the other sea scouts, and it became our quest when we cruised for girls in Brooklyn's Prospect Park. We were looking for what were then called "Victory Girls," young women willing to sacrifice everything for young men going off to war.

We pretended to be sailors. There were only two differences between our uniforms and the Navy's: the anchors on the back corners of our collars instead of stars, and over the front left pocket the letters *B.S.A.* to identify us as Boy Scouts of America. When some of the girls questioned our lack of height, we explained that we were sub-mariners, and when they asked what *B.S.A.* referred to, we told them, "Battle Squadron A."

None of them ever questioned the anchors.

We picked up lots of patriotic V-Girls in Prospect Park, but unlike some of the more experienced and handsome sea scouts, I couldn't find one willing to sacrifice everything for my sake.

"I wish I could join the Navy too," I said to Stretch, as we took the elevator up to our lockers that morning at NYU, "but with my bad vision, I guess it's the infantry for me."

"You can always join the Maritime Service. They don't have high physical requirements, and Merchant Marine duty would exempt you from the draft."

"I guess that way I'd still be serving my country."

"Sure. Considering the mines and torpedoes, it's hazardous duty. I read somewhere that more merchant seamen were killed on the Murmansk run than Navy sailors."

We took our lab coats from our lockers and headed for class. "My folks would never sign the papers."

"They would if you explained the alternative."

As we entered the biology lab, and each moved to our different sections, I was surprised at the smell of formaldehyde. On the marble worktable in front of each student's station lay a covered tray. I reached out to uncover it, but the prof's voice called out: *"Do not touch the tray in front of you!"*

His lab assistant was moving from student to student dropping off a rolled-up dissection kit and a pair of rubber gloves in front of each tray. When he was done, the prof called out, "Put on the gloves and then uncover the trays."

I peeled back the cover, startled to see a dead white mouse on its side.

"Today," he announced, "you will dissect a real specimen."

I knew the bio lab required dissection, but I'd expected a warning. Obviously, the professor enjoyed springing this as a surprise on his students. Not that it bothered me. I was taking bio as a premed requirement because I was going to be a surgeon.

In the Boy Scouts I had taken the Advanced First Aid Merit Badge, and in the Sea Scouts during cruises, I was considered "ship's doctor." I treated wounds, boils, and abrasions and had become used to the sight and smell of blood. I had hardened myself.

On one *Dutchman* weekend trip up the East River, the crew nearly mutinied over the terrible meals. Since I'd held part-time jobs as a sandwich man in a luncheonette, I was drafted into being ship's cook as well. The joke on that voyage was that if I didn't kill them as doctor I'd poison them as cook.

Dissecting a mouse would be no problem.

"Open your dissection kits." He pulled down a chart in front of the blackboard. It showed a mouse's internal organs. "Now, with the scalpel, make an incision in your specimen from the neck through the abdomen to the tail, then pull the skin back with the forceps."

I followed his instructions. The incision was quick and neat and revealed that my specimen was female.

"Proceed to remove the organs, placing them into the petri dishes, and labeling each one."

My specimen's uterus was distended. I cut it open, stared in disbelief, and backed away from the table. It contained a cluster of tiny fetuses curled up, eyes shut.

"You look pale," my neighbor across the table said. "What's the matter?"

What had startled me at first now saddened me. Several tiny lives had been snuffed out so that I could have a hands-on dissection experience.

A young woman on my left leaned forward to look. Before I could catch her she fainted, knocking over her stool with a loud crash. The lab assistant rushed to revive her with smelling salts, and the prof told us to continue dissections on our own as he and his assistant took her to the infirmary.

But I, great surgeon-to-be, was paralyzed. The thought of removing the fetuses sickened me. I dashed out of the lab into the lavatory, washed my face and hands, and stared at myself in the mirror. I had to go back and finish what I'd started.

After a few minutes, I returned to the lab.

Embarrassed at having fled, I covered up my overreaction by blurting out, "As the proud godfather of a litter, I'm handing out cigarettes in lieu of cigars."

Laughter, pats on the back, and mock congratulations steadied me, but as I finished the dissection a jingle went through my mind:

> *Three blind mice, see how they run.*
> *They all run after the farmer's wife,*
> *Who cut off their tails with a carving knife.*
> *You never saw such a sight in your life,*
> *As three blind mice.*

"Good job," the prof said, as he examined my work. "I'm giving you an A."

On the way out, Stretch punched me playfully. "Lucky guy, getting the pregnant one."

That night, as I opened my English Lit anthology for the next day's quiz on British poets, I scanned the table of contents and saw *Algernon Charles Swinburne.* I thought, What an unusual first name.

3

||||||||||||||||||||||||||

SECOND ACTING

ALTHOUGH I'D ALWAYS WANTED to become a writer, I wasn't sure what kind of writing. After I read Nathanael West's horror story of Hollywood—*The Day of the Locust*—I ruled out screenwriting.

That left plays, short stories, or novels. I'd read hundreds of each, but my only experience with live theater were student performances in school. I was on stage once, in third grade, and I played an oracle. In a deep voice, full of portent, I said to the king of the Aztecs, "Thy days are numbered, Montezuma."

That was the extent of my acting experience.

In my teens, I glorified Manhattan. It was Baghdad-on-the-Hudson, city of the arts, of publishing, and Broadway theater. I could reach that mecca for a nickel, and see two-thirds of a show free of charge. All I had to do was mingle with the crowd that stepped out for a smoke after the first-act curtain. When the buzzer announced the second-act warning, I would drift in among them and quickly find a seat before the lights dimmed. I called it *second acting*.

The year was 1942. I was fifteen, and the play was *The Skin of Our Teeth*. Since I had read *Our Town* in high school, and seen the movie, the thought of second acting a Thornton Wilder play excited me.

I was clever enough never to try it on weekends. On a mid-week evening, I put on my navy blue suit, a conservative tie, and took the subway to Times Square. I was early that night, as I walked to the theater district, so I lingered outside Lindy's Restaurant for a while and peered through the window. I imagined Damon Runyon's hustlers, gamblers, and gangsters, guys and dolls hanging out at the restaurant. Runyon called it *Mindy's*. When I could afford to splurge, I'd go inside, sit near the window looking out at the Broadway passersby, and gorge myself on the cheesecake Runyon had immortalized.

I stopped daydreaming and focused on the task at hand. I didn't mind missing the first act of *The Skin of Our Teeth*. I could usually figure out the opening situation, but even if I couldn't, it didn't matter. I would develop the opening in my mind, write a beginning that brought the characters and the story together. In those days, I saw many second and third acts, but never any firsts.

Always after the final curtain, I would applaud with the others, and visualize the glories of a playwright's life. Curtain calls on opening night of a smash hit. Shouts of "Author! Author!" Bows and bouquets. Then to Sardi's for celebration with champagne and caviar as everyone waited for the early *Times* review.

That night started out the same as usual. I blended in with the crowd of smokers that spilled out of the theater onto the sidewalk, took a cigarette from my imitation gold case, and lit up. I mingled with the paying customers and listened to the chatter about the first act, picking up clues about the opening.

When the second-act warning buzzer sounded, I merged with them into the lobby. Above their heads, I caught a glimpse of the faces of Fredric March and Tallulah Bankhead on the life-sized poster. I'd seen them both in the movies, of course. Tonight, I would see them live, on stage, in a Thornton Wilder play.

Once inside, I hung back at the rear, scanning the rows for an empty seat, ready to slide into it before the lights dimmed. I saw two in the center off the aisle, but as I made my move I was jostled aside by the latecomers.

Only then did I realize that the crowd was larger than usual. I moved to the wall, peering through the dimming light, my eyes growing used to the dark. Every seat was occupied. Did I dare try the balcony? I'd come this far. Might as well. I went back and headed upstairs two steps at a time. I found a *Playbill,* slipped it into my jacket pocket, and headed for an empty seat in the center of a row.

As I sat down, a woman glared at me. "What are you doing? That's my husband's seat!"

"Sorry," I said. "Wrong row."

I jumped up and squeezed my way back to the aisle as a huge man headed toward me. I'd waited too long. I had to backtrack to the other end. People grumbled as I stepped on their feet.

An usher with a flashlight was waiting for me. "May I see your ticket stub? The curtain is about to go up."

Heart pounding, I pretended to search my pockets. "I must have dropped it somewhere. I had it right here."

She looked at me suspiciously. "There are no empty seats in the balcony."

"I'll go down to the lobby and see if I can find it."

"Let me light your way."

"Not necessary," I whispered, moving quickly. But I missed the last step and fell.

"Sir, are you hurt? Let me take you to the manager's office."

"No. No. That's all right. I'm fine."

I ran down the steps two at a time into the empty lobby. There I saw the full length of the poster with a banner announcement that had been hidden by the crowd heading inside for the second act: *TONIGHT'S PERFORMANCE SOLD OUT!*

Stupid! Stupid! Stupid!

Out of the lobby, into the street. Only then did I look back at the marquee at the play's title that now mocked my close call. THE SKIN OF OUR TEETH.

I walked north on Broadway to Central Park South, telling myself I might find an adventure along the way. Since it was late, I didn't enter the park, just sat on one of the benches and looked up at the luxury hotels. The name Essex House impressed me and I wondered about the lives of wealthy people who lived there. Someday, I would look down from one of those windows to where I was sitting now.

As I passed the theater district on the way back to the subway, I saw the street filled with the exiting theater crowd. Some people entered waiting limos or hailed taxis. Others walked toward brightly lit Broadway.

Once again, I merged into the crowd, as if by being among them I could be part of them. Many held the *Playbill* in their hands. I pulled mine out of my pocket, and held it as a badge that showed I belonged in their world.

One group turned off into Sardi's. I followed them in and looked around. After they were seated, I saw the head waiter approach. I waved my *Playbill* at him and asked for directions to the men's room.

When I left Sardi's and continued on to the subway, I tried to imagine what the play I had not seen might be like. I couldn't. So on the ride back to Brooklyn, I made one up, about a boy who had a great adventure, a narrow escape—by the skin of his teeth—as he tried to second act a Broadway play.

Twenty-five years later, in 1967, I received a fellowship to the MacDowell Colony for Creative Artists in Peterborough, New Hampshire to work on my second novel *The Touch*.

I was assigned a luxurious studio deep in the woods. On the first day, I was told that to preserve solitude for creativity, the only distraction would occur at noon each day when a car would drive up the gravel path and someone would leave my lunch basket at the door.

Exploring the studio, I noticed a piece of wood in the shape of a paddle on the fireplace mantel. It was inscribed with a list of names of former visitors, some at the top faded, others at the bottom fresh. As I glanced up the long list, I saw the name: *Thornton Wilder*. In 1936 or 1937 he had written *Our Town* in the same studio where I would be working on *The Touch* for the next month.

Remembering my failed evening at the theater, I added my name at the bottom of the paddle.

4

||||||||||||||||||||

BREAKING DISHES

IT WAS OBVIOUS TO ME in my youth that my parents wouldn't be able to send me to college, much less medical school. If I was to get a higher education, I would have to work and save.

During summer vacations, when I was eight or nine, I quickly graduated from street corner lemonade stands to selling soda pop and sandwiches. I bought rye bread and salami at a delicatessen and made sandwiches. I bought bottles of soda pop from a nearby wholesaler and packed them in ice in my little red wagon. I sold lunches to women who worked in a garment factory on Van Sinderen Avenue, the borderline between Brownsville and East New York.

I did very well until I was squeezed out by the owner of the delicatessen. Able to gauge my success by the increase in the size of my orders, he put his nephew to work on my route, undercut my prices, and drove me out of business.

In the years that followed, I delivered tuxedos for weddings, assembled screwdrivers in a factory, and worked the first *frozen custard* machine in Brownsville. None of them paid much, but I had to save for college.

Two other jobs that I stored away in what I later called my mental root cellar—working as a baker's boy, and later as waiter in a luncheonette—stayed hidden in deep memory until *Flowers for Algernon* needed them.

When I was fourteen, I went to work as a deliveryman's assistant for the East New York Bagel Bakery, beneath the elevated train, around the corner from where I lived. To start at four in the morning, I had to get up at three A.M. I worked until seven A.M. until the driver dropped me off at Junior High School 149. Out of school at three in the afternoon, homework, dinner, and then to bed while it was still daylight.

At first, my job was to help the driver load the back of his van with baskets of hot bagels, some plain, some with poppy or sesame seeds, some with salt. I would sit beside him in the passenger seat while we drove to groceries and restaurants that had not yet opened for business.

As we approached each location in the predawn hours, the driver consulted his order list and called out the size of the order. "Two dozen. One plain, one poppy."

The back of the passenger seat had been removed, so I would turn, grasp three still-hot bagels in each hand, and call out "Six! A dozen! Six! Two dozen!" There were no *baker's dozens* then. Poppy- and sesame-seed bagels were painful because they scraped my fingers. But the salt-covered bagels hurt most of all when they touched my raw skin. I bagged them, and as the driver pulled to the curb I jumped out and left them in still-dark doorways.

I remember the day he changed the route to deliver to a new customer. As we passed the corner of Livonia and Saratoga avenues, I saw lights on in a candy store. "That's strange," I said. "Maybe it's being robbed."

He laughed. "Midnight Rose is open twenty-four hours a day. Nobody in his right mind would rob that store."

When I asked why, he shook his head and said it wasn't too

smart to ask questions about the wiseguys who hung out at Midnight Rose's place.

At about this time, I got to know an older boy whose family moved in across the street from my home on Snediker Avenue. He was training to become a boxer, he said, but since he was actually too young to box, he confided in me that he planned to use his older brother's nickname, "Kid Twist." He would fight as "The Kid."

I told him I wished I had enough money to pay for the Atlas Dynamic Tension Method so that I could put on muscles like Mr. Atlas in the magazines and comic books and learn to defend myself against some of the bullies who picked on me.

The Kid weight-lifted at the Adonis Club on Livonia Avenue, and one day he took me with him and introduced me around. Some of the musclemen laughed when they saw how skinny I was, but they were very polite to The Kid, and gave me advice on how to pump iron. I see them clearly in my mind now, standing in front of mirrors after lifting weights, flexing oiled muscles, the smell of sweat filling the air.

Hoboes dropped in from time to time, to wash up and sometimes to sleep in the back for a night or two. I listened with fascination at their stories of hopping freight trains across the country and meeting old friends with strange names at hobo camps. I thought of quitting school and hopping a freight in the nearby rail yards to see America. Then I'd have something to write about.

Later, I learned about "Kid" Reles's brother. I still have the newspaper clip from November 13, 1941.

ABE RELES KILLED TRYING TO ESCAPE
Abe "Kid Twist" Reles, a major hit man for a murder-for-hire ring, had been testifying against his confederates, and the

Mafia who used their services. Early...Wednesday, November 12, 1941, although closely guarded by five detectives, Abe Reles either jumped, fell or was pushed out of the sixth floor window of the Half Moon Hotel on the Coney Island boardwalk. Reporters dubbed him "the canary that could sing but couldn't fly."

Then I understood what the bagel delivery driver had told me about the men who hung out at Midnight Rose's Candy Store. They were the Mafia's execution squad, and reporters called them *"Murder Inc."*

The killers operated right in my neighborhood, and received their hit contracts from the bosses in Manhattan who phoned them at the candy store. My boxer friend's brother, Abe "Kid Twist" Reles, had been one of their most feared killers. Shortly after the article appeared, my friend and his family moved from the neighborhood without warning, and I never saw him again.

I was soon promoted from the bagel delivery van to an inside job as baker's helper. Later, when I was practicing writing scenes from my own experiences, I wrote a brief sketch of my impressions of the bakery. Here, unedited, is that memory.

The bagel factory—the smell of raw dough, and the whitened floors and walls...working and kneading the dough in circular motions. Rolling it into long thin tubes, and then with a quick twist of the wrist making them into little circles...another [baker] laying these out neatly in a huge shallow wooden tray...stacking them high...to be wheeled over to the urn and oven. There a boy stands lifting them out of the tray three at a time and throwing them into the bubbling urn...then scooping them out, dripping and slimy, with a wire net...dumping them on the baker's table. The baker spreads them neatly along the long wooden oar, slides them into the kiln, leaving long deep rows of bagels on wooden paddles while he fills up the next oar...Pulls out an oar covered with browned bagels, and runs a string along beneath the bagels to separate them from the wood...finally, dumping them into huge wicker baskets where they will be taken out into the waiting truck for delivery in the early dawn. The baker with the lame foot...the one who has the rasping voice...

Many years later, I used that setting in the novel version of *Flowers for Algernon.*

The night shift at the bakery interfered with sleep and study and my grades suffered, so I took a job as dishwasher in Parkie's ice-cream parlor on Sutter Avenue. He soon promoted me to soda jerk, then to sandwich maker, counterman, and short-order cook. At sixteen, I found a better job on Pitkin Avenue, a more prestigious location near the Lowes' Pitkin Theater, to wait tables in Meyer's Goody Shoppe.

There was no longer a Meyer at Meyer's Goody Shoppe. The luncheonette and ice-cream parlor was owned by Mr. Goldstein and Mr. Sohn, both of whom nearly drove all us waiters crazy.

Sweet and gentle Mr. Goldstein always spoke of his desire to help poor boys who were working their way through college. Near the entrance, on the wall behind the cash register, he'd hung photographs from former waiters who had, as he said, "made good." Some were in Army, Navy or Marine uniforms. Others were wearing graduation robes. Goldstein spoke of "his boys" with affection. When I had first applied for the job, and told him my parents wanted me to go to medical school, he patted my head, and said I was a good boy to listen to my parents.

During the nights he was on duty, if business was slow, he was calm and would sit at the counter and discuss issues of the day with the idle short-order cooks. But when things got busy, he became transformed. Reflective Mr. Goldstein became a screamer, shouting orders at us over the customers' heads.

Mr. Sohn was a different sort of character. When business was good, he stuck to the cash register. We were free to handle our tables in quiet dignity. But during slow periods, before the crowds came in, or between the dinner rush and the after-movie rush, Mr. Sohn would slip into the dining room and, under the pretext of inspecting our stations, he would take possession of most sugar dispensers, ketchup bottles, and saltshakers and hide them on the shelves below the cash register.

One of the veteran waiters explained that it was Sohn's reaction to one traumatic day when vandals had emptied all the saltshakers into the sugar dispensers. Sohn was also convinced that someone was stealing knives, forks, and spoons, and he intended to find the culprit. He made frequent sorties from behind the cash register to the dishwasher's station and removed much of the flatware. This led to a shortage of every kind of cutlery whenever Sohn was on duty.

At first, it created intense rivalry among the waiters. None of us wanted to tell our customers there were no spoons for their ice cream and coffee, no forks for their chocolate cake. Irate customers would storm out without tipping and without paying, and it was no use trying to explain to Sohn that it was his fault.

I learned from the veterans how to survive. During Sohn nights we prepared ourselves by slipping flatware into our pockets, under our belts, and beneath our shirts. We occasionally joined forces to divert Sohn's attention, and penetrated his fortress to liberate sugar, ketchup, and salt.

Quiet Sohn and *Screaming Goldstein* kept us waiters on our toes—sometimes on each other's toes.

In the two years I'd worked there, I accumulated enough tips for my first year's tuition at NYU. Then one evening my life turned a corner.

The after-movie crowd started arriving at ten o'clock. The place filled up quickly, and soon there was a crowd waiting outside. When four couples arrived and broke through the line, Goldstein did something I'd never seen before. He greeted them, smiling and fawning, led them past the other protesting customers, and directed them to my station.

As I went to get water and menus, Goldstein suddenly showed up with glasses of water on a tray. "How come there are no napkins on the tables?" he shouted at me. "Where's the silverware? Why don't they have menus?"

"Mr. Goldstein, they just sat down."

Explaining was useless, so I tried to ignore him as I took their orders. He bustled around, smiling at them. A few minutes later, when he passed me near the kitchen, he said, "What's taking you so long?"

"I just put my orders in, Mr. Goldstein."

"They're ready. On the counter."

I turned to look, and sure enough, the normally lethargic countermen had gone into action and given my new customers' orders of sandwiches and waffles priority.

"What's going on?" I asked one of the older waiters.

"Give 'em good service," he whispered. "Those guys hang out at Midnight Rose's."

I carried two cups of coffee with glass creamers balanced on the edges of the saucers in my left hand, and three sandwiches and waffles spread across my right arm.

Goldstein again reappeared from between two aisles. "What's taking you so long?"

"I'm delivering their orders."

"These are special customers."

"I've figured that out already. Mr. Goldstein, please give me a chance..."

He blocked my path. "Watch those creamers!"

I looked, and saw that my trembling hands were making the glass creamers alongside the coffee cups jiggle on the edges of the saucers. He walked backward, facing me, shouting at me. The more he shouted, the more they jiggled. I had learned that a glass creamer, if dropped, would break on the third bounce. If you could kick it to one side before that, you could prevent it from shattering.

Jiggle. Jiggle. One dropped, and bounced twice. I tried to kick it aside before the third hit, but failed. It shattered. I attempted to block-kick the second creamer: Bounce...bounce... *break!* By now I was off balance and the sandwich plates nestled along my right arm wobbled. I tried to grab them but it was too late. Everything else I was carrying crashed to the floor.

"Mazel tov!" someone shouted, amid laughter. Then a couple of others took up the cry, laughing and applauding as if I were a bridegroom stomping the wineglass at a wedding. Someone called out, "The kid ain't stupid! That's better than washing them!"

Goldstein's face turned red and menacing. "What's the matter with you?" He addressed the mocking customers. "A college boy, and he can't even wait on tables." And then to me, "Clean it up, moron!"

His expression of disgust said it all. He'd given me a chance to work because I needed money for college, and I had betrayed him by breaking his dishes in front of his special customers. He walked away and didn't speak to me for the rest of the evening. But my Murder, Inc. customers left me big tips.

At closing time, I finished cleaning up, refilling sugar bowls and ketchup bottles and mopping the floors around my tables. Then I went up to him and said, "Good-bye, Mr. Goldstein. I'll send you a photograph for your *mailing* wall as a token of my appreciation."

His brow furrowed. "What do you mean?"

"You've helped me make a decision. I can't put up with this crap anymore. I'm enlisting in the Merchant Marine."

"What about college?"

"That'll have to wait until after the war is over."

He looked at me long and hard. His voice was cold as he said, "Good luck." And as I headed for the door, he shouted so that everyone would hear, "Hey, moron!"

I didn't turn.

"Hey, smart college boy!"

I looked back at him.

"Try not to break everything on the ship!"

That's how, years later, I could imagine what Charlie Gordon felt during the scene in a restaurant when he sees a mentally handicapped busboy drop and break a tray of dishes, and the owner shouts: *"All right, you dope, don't just stand there! Get a broom and sweep that mess up. A broom... a broom, you idiot!"*

Suddenly, I was furious at myself and all those who were smirking at him. I wanted to pick up the dishes and throw them. I wanted to smash their laughing faces. I jumped up and shouted: "Shut up! Leave him alone! He can't understand. He can't help what he is... but for God's sake, have some respect! He's a human being!"

I was able to see it through Charlie's eyes and feel his emotions. I was able to write it, because it happened to me.

5

||||||||||||||||||||||||

I BECOME SHIP'S DOCTOR

I KNEW THAT JOINING the U.S. Maritime Service would be a turning point. I would be away from my parents, living my own life, pursuing my own dreams. But because I was three months short of my eighteenth birthday, to enlist I needed one of my parents' signatures.

My mother insisted that I was too young, too thin, too short, and too nearsighted.

"They don't care," I said. "I can pass the physical."

My father asked, "What about college?"

"A lot of other guys are in the same boat, Dad. They enacted a new law last year—the G.I. Bill—to pay college tuition for servicemen. After my discharge, I'll be able to continue my education free of charge."

I didn't know at the time that Maritime Service duty would not make me eligible for G.I. benefits.

"You'll still become a doctor?" she asked. "Doctors save lives."

"Of course, I'll become a doctor."

My father frowned. "What about that writer stuff?"

I told them about Somerset Maugham and Chekhov and

Conan Doyle having been physicians who later became famous authors, and that I wasn't foolish enough to believe I'd be able to support myself by writing. I didn't mention that as doctors, my three heroes had failed.

"Practicing medicine will be my profession," I said. "Writing will be my hobby."

"You're only seventeen," my mother sobbed. "You're still my baby."

I thought, but didn't tell them that, at seventeen, Jack London had shipped out for a year on a seal hunting schooner and later used his adventures to write *The Sea Wolf.* I believed that, like London, writing of my own seafaring experiences would launch my career as an author, but what I said was, "I promise I'll be a doctor."

My father signed the enlistment papers, and set me free.

After six weeks of basic training at Sheepshead Bay, I was transferred to Radio Officers' Training School on Hoffman Island, in New York Harbor. I liked the thought of sending messages in Morse code and being called *Sparks.* Perhaps that would be my pen name.

My only memory of Hoffman Island is meeting Morton Klass, who was to become my lifelong friend. Our last names began with K, and so we marched, ate, and sat in classes side by side. Since Mort's bunk was across from mine, we argued politics, philosophy, and literature, often long after lights-out, until some of the men threw their boots across the barracks to shut us up.

After Germany surrendered on May 7, 1945, the U.S. Maritime Service discovered they had a surplus of radio operators and closed the Hoffman Island Radio Officers' School. Mort sailed as an engine room wiper, and I was shipped out a week later to

Le Havre, as Army utility aboard a luxury liner that had been converted into a troopship.

My ship traveled back and forth to France carrying fresh troops to the replacement depot—the men called it *repo depo*—and bringing back G.I.'s who had completed their European tours of duty. They slept in bunks stacked five high in the hold that reeked of sweat, booze, and vomit. The poker games went on twenty-four hours a day.

Shore leave in Le Havre was short, and all I remember is the mud and destruction and poverty—images I stored away.

After my second voyage on the troopship, I learned that, although the War Shipping Administration had a surplus of radio officers, there was a shortage of pursers. They put out a call for seamen with clerical experience.

As it turned out, one of the most useful courses I had taken in junior high school was touch-typing. Long before it helped me as a writer, I had been able to get clerical jobs during summer breaks. With recommendations from former employers, and a successful series of tests, I was granted a purser's license from the War Shipping Administration.

Now, with a U.S. Maritime Service rank of ensign, I no longer wore bell-bottoms. A staff officer's uniform with crossed quills above one gold stripe on each sleeve designated my rating. Instead of being called *Sparks,* I would be called purser.

Planning to write of my experiences, I changed the name of the ship and the shipping company in the records I kept, and I avoided using the real names of officers and crew. Except for those changes, what follows really happened.

My first duties as ship's purser took place at the New York office of International Tankers, Inc., where I drew up the ship's manifest and crew lists for the S.S. *Polestar* and supervised the men's signing of ship's articles in the presence of the shipping commissioner.

The Navy told us only that it was to be a short coastwise voyage. When I questioned one company official, he pointed to a sign on the office wall showing a flaming ship disappearing into the ocean. Beneath it were the words: A SLIP OF THE LIP CAN SINK A SHIP.

The men and I were told only that the *Polestar* would depart some time within the next two days from Bayonne, New Jersey, and that I would meet the captain—now on leave to visit his family in Philadelphia—just before sailing. As a matter of security, I learned, we would not be informed of the port of call or the duration of the voyage until after the tugs had escorted us out of New York Harbor and the harbor pilot had left the ship. Only after we were out to sea would the captain open his sailing orders and inform us of our destination.

It was a freezing January morning in 1946 when I finally got to the Bayonne docks. The taxi pulled up as close to the pier as possible, and I made my way along the ice-caked earth, stepping over networks of pipes, and ducking under suspended hoses that creaked and swayed in their slings. Finally, I made out the name of my T-2 tanker at the end of the dock—S.S. *Polestar.*

Empty of cargo, the ship rode high, looming over the dock, and the gangway tilted up at a forty-five-degree angle. Slipping one of my bags under my arm, I grabbed the railing and climbed up to the well deck. It was littered with papers and empty beer cans. The smell of oil was overpowering, and I had to stop at the windward side for swallows of air before climbing the ladder to the main deck. I could hear the ship creaking as she rose and fell with the wash. Other than that no sounds. It felt like a ghost ship.

I found my way to the purser's cabin, unpacked and stowed my books: Homer, Plato, and Shakespeare, as well as *War and*

Peace and *Moby Dick* in the rack above the desk. Hearing a rustling, I turned to see a baby-faced officer leaning against the open door, watching me. He had four gold stripes on his sleeves.

"Welcome aboard, Purser. I see you're a reader."

"Yes, Captain."

"We have a pretty good ship's library. You'll be in charge of lending out books. Mostly donations, of course, but if there are any special books you want let me know. We have a petty cash fund."

"Glad to hear that."

"But I think you should check out the dispensary and ship's hospital in case you need to order any additional medication or supplies. The last purser was pretty lackadaisical, and he was always running out of stuff."

"Ship's hospital? I don't understand. What's that got to do with me?"

He glanced at my jacket hanging over the back of the chair and frowned, pointing to my sleeve embroidered with gold braid crossed quills. "Where's the caduceus?"

Then I realized he was referring to the winged staff entwined with a snake which, along with crossed quills, would have denoted the usual dual rating of purser/pharmacist mate.

"I'm a purser, Captain, but not a pharmacist mate."

His face reddened. "I told the shipping commissioner I needed a replacement purser who was also a medic!"

"They told me there's a shortage of pursers, especially purser/pharmacist mates. That's why they hired me."

"This won't do, Keyes. I've got forty men aboard ship whose medical needs must be attended to."

Without thinking of the consequences, I blurted out, "I've got First Aid Expert merit badges in both the Boy Scouts and Sea

Scouts. I served as ship's doctor on a few of our sailing trips. I was premed at college, and I'm planning to become a surgeon."

He studied me for a long time. "Okay, Keyes. You'll have to do. As soon as we're at sea—beyond coastal limits—I'll use my authority to designate you our pharmacist mate. In addition to your regular purser's duties, you'll run the dispensary and hospital, handle sick call, and do short-arm inspections after every shore leave."

"But, Captain—"

"No *but*s about it! You're ship's doctor." On his way out, he asked, "Play chess?"

"Yes, sir."

"How good?"

"Average."

"Fine. We'll have a game tonight after dinner."

When he was gone, I slumped on my settee. Me and my big mouth. Wrapping and taping down bandages and dispensing aspirin on a Sea Scout weekend voyage up the East River was a far cry from being a physician to forty men at sea.

I beat the captain at chess that evening, but when I saw the annoyance in his blue eyes, I decided not to let that happen too often.

Next morning, the throbbing engines woke me, and I rushed out on deck to watch us weigh anchor and leave port. But I was too late. I climbed one of the ladders to an empty guntub, where antiaircraft cannon had once been mounted, and from that position I could scan the horizon all around me. Unlike sailing along the East River on the *Dutchman III,* now there was no land in sight anywhere.

Suddenly, I had cast off all earthbound duties, plans, responsibilities. Worries and conflicts sloughed off like dead skin, giving way to deep relaxation. Without land in sight, there was no reality—no life, no death—nothing of importance but the here and now of the sea.

For the first time in my life, surrounded by sky and water I experienced "the oceanic feeling," and I understood why men, like an old seaman I'd visited in Sailors' Snug Harbor, followed the sea.

At sixteen, shortly after I had joined the Sea Scouts, I'd made a pilgrimage to the old sailors' home in Staten Island that provided a haven for retired seamen. There I visited one weather-beaten old salt. We sat in the visiting room silently for a while smoking our pipes, I in my pressed Sea Scout uniform and crisp peacoat, he with his black watch cap and threadbare peacoat pulled tight against the drafts.

Then, gripping my wrist, and fixing me with his rheumy-eyed stare, he reminisced about his seafaring days. Images from "The Rime of the Ancient Mariner" flooded my mind: *He holds him with his skinny hand... He holds him with his glittering eye—*

Like the Ancient Mariner, my old sailor held me captive as he described how his ship had been blown off course, and was then becalmed among the gulfweed drifting in currents into the great whirl in the North Atlantic to which all the sargasso weed in the world flowed. It was known as the Sargasso Sea.

"The island of lost ships and lost souls," he said.

He spoke of ships trapped in the weeds, as well as wrecked vessels that drifted into this watery graveyard, with crews of corpses waiting to be freed from the sargasso weed. He spoke of his own crew surviving there on the worms and tiny crabs, shrimps and octopuses that had changed color and shape, taking on camouflage to look like the floating, bulbous seaweed they lived on. Of mosquitoes big as birds.

"That's where the eels return to," he said, "millions of slimy snakes of the sea, from thousands of miles, from faraway waters coming back to mate, spawn, and die."

He was a good storyteller, and I sat there spellbound, listening to him for a long time, pipe smoke curling between us. Then he nodded off to sleep, and I slipped away.

Looking at the ocean now from the deck of the *Polestar* I felt lonely and sad, and then an idea surfaced. In "The Rime of the Ancient Mariner," Coleridge must have been describing the Sargasso when he wrote:

> *We were the first that ever burst*
> *Into that silent sea....*

and

> *Yea, slimy things did crawl with legs*
> *Upon the slimy sea.*

The engines throbbing beneath my feet brought me back to reality. I turned away from the railing, climbed down from the guntub, and crossed the catwalk to the officers' dining saloon.

There, at breakfast, I was introduced to the chief mate who looked like a wrestler, and to the chief engineer, a huge, red-faced Georgian who sported pearl-handled six-guns, and to Sparks, the radio operator, whose eyes stared in different directions.

The captain informed us that he had opened the Navy's sealed orders. "The *Polestar*'s destination is Aruba," he said. "There we take on bunkers for our own fuel supply. Then to Caracas, loading a full cargo of Venezuelan heating oil and off-loading it in Philadelphia. Expected duration of voyage, three weeks."

After breakfast, he motioned for me to stay behind.

"The men will get overnight shore leave in Aruba, and two days in Caracas," he said. "The last purser was supposed to lay in a good supply of condoms and prophylaxis ointment kits, but he slipped up. Normally, you'd conduct short-arm inspection for gonorrhea after the men come back aboard from each port, but since most of the crew signed on again in New York, you'd better do your first short-arm tomorrow."

I reminded him that he was to officially appoint me ship's doctor.

"Consider yourself so appointed."

I thought a moment. "I'd like it in writing, Captain."

He glared at me. "Eh?" Which I mentally translated as, *Smart-Ass.*

But then he softened, scribbled a note on a napkin, and handed it to me. I folded it carefully and put it into my wallet for safekeeping beside my staff officer's papers.

Several of the men showed the green-pus symptoms of gonorrhea, and I put them on a regimen of penicillin shots every four hours around the clock for two days. For the night shots, I had to go down to the men's quarters with a flashlight, shine it into their eyes to waken them, and roll them over. I gave each one a slap on the butt before punching in the needle, and few of them felt it going in.

I splinted one man's broken left arm—a simple fracture that could be set after we returned to the States.

My other duties included once-a-week openings of the slop chest for candy, cigarettes, and sundries. We were running low on most supplies so I had to ration them. It confirmed what the captain had said about the last purser. He'd been sloppy about provisioning the slop chest.

Other than medical duties and tending the store, I was financial officer. I would have to give the men a draw, advancing them local currency for shore leave in each port. To prevent them from jumping ship in midvoyage, the advance was limited to one-half the money they'd already earned. All I needed to do was multiply each man's rate of pay by the number of days at sea. They could draw up to one-half that amount. I couldn't begin to calculate the draw until the captain told me the date of arrival.

That left me lots of time to read and write. I used my office typewriter to try my hand at writing sketches from my past and keeping my personal journal for material to store away for the sea novel I knew I would write someday.

I realized I had to train myself in the craft of writing. I had studied every book on the subject I could get my hands on. Somerset Maugham, in his autobiographical *The Summing Up,* describes how he taught himself to write by spending days in the library copying passages of authors he admired. That shocked me, at first, but then I understood. Now, with books from the ship's library, I did the same.

I believed that, like Maugham, I would eventually outgrow imitation, but by then I would have learned to shape words into sentences, and to mold them into paragraphs. I trusted myself to develop an ear for language, and to find my own voice and personal style, as well as those of my characters. Since Maugham hadn't been too proud to learn to write as children do—by imitation—neither was I.

From Hemingway, I learned to write simple declarative sentences devoid of figures of speech, in the down-to-earth, transparent style he had learned from Mark Twain. *Huckleberry Finn,* Hemingway said, is the book from which all American fiction descended, and I believe it was the poet Archibald MacLeish who said that Hemingway had fashioned "a style for his time," playing on the title of Hemingway's first published collection of short stories, *In Our Time.*

From Faulkner, I learned to break those chains, freeing myself to write long, complex sentences and parenthetical paragraphs, often with imagery that explodes into metaphor.

Eventually, I weaned myself from both of them.

In the beginning of "Flowers for Algernon," Charlie's style is direct, childlike, and free of metaphors, but as he changes, his simple declarative sentences become compound and then complex, then intricate and metaphoric. As his ability to write deteriorates, his style becomes simple again, until he reverts to near illiteracy.

I learned from the masters in the ship's library.

After refueling in Aruba, the *Polestar* sailed to Caracas for a cargo of heating oil. Then we were homeward bound, with little for me to do until the captain gave me our arrival date in Philadelphia.

Sparks and I were playing chess in my office when, suddenly, there was a furious banging at my door, and a distraught seaman burst into my cabin. "Purser! Come quick! Something's wrong with one of the deckhands."

"What is it?"

"I dunno, but he's been puking, and now there's dark stuff coming out of his mouth and nose."

I grabbed my black bag and shouted to Sparks to alert the captain or chief mate. Then I followed the seaman along the catwalk to the men's quarters on the forward deck. A crowd outside the fo'c'sle parted to make way for me. As I reached the doorway and smelled a mixture of sweet lemony syrup and vomit, I started to gag, but I braced myself and went inside.

A heavyset man was lying on his back across a bottom bunk, with his head halfway to the deck, his face covered with dark, bloody ooze. He was sucking it in and out of his nostrils and mouth, gurgling and gasping for air.

I had seen this middle-aged seaman, from time to time, mopping oil from the well deck, or on a scaffold over the side, painting or chipping. He'd come to the dispensary a couple of times for aspirin to dull his hangovers, and once he mentioned a large family in Philadelphia.

I had no idea what was wrong with him, but I realized he was drowning in his own blood-filled vomit.

"Help me roll him over!"

Two men jumped forward and we turned him facedown to keep him from choking.

"Anyone know what happened? What's that sweet smell?"

"He ran out of booze after we left Caracas," one of the seamen said. "Broke into the galley after Cookie closed it, and stole a quart of lemon extract. I think he drank it all."

I shook my head. What was I going to do? Even facedown, he was still choking, sucking fluid back up his nose.

Sparks showed up. "What a stink! Need help, Purse?"

"Get the captain!"

"Orders not to wake him. First mate's on watch in the wheelhouse."

"This guy's drowning in his own bloody vomit. I'll give him artificial respiration, to see if I can clear his lungs. Get on the radio and try to contact the nearest Navy ship with a doctor aboard. Tell them this guy drank a quart of lemon extract."

Sparks nodded and dashed out.

I took off my shoes, straddled the seaman, and turned his head to the left. Then I began pumping him as I'd learned in the Sea Scouts.

"Out goes the bad air..." pressing down on his back. "In comes the good air..." releasing to let the lungs fill. "Out goes the bad air...in comes the good air."

I sat astride him for nearly half an hour, pumping and releasing, wondering if I was helping him or killing him.

A messman showed up with a radio message Sparks had received from a Navy ship. It read, *"Give artificial respiration."*

I felt better knowing I was doing the right thing. I showed one of the seamen how to spell me, and he began by imitating

my movements, and then taking over. "Out goes the bad air...
In comes the good..."

When I could no longer find a pulse, I sent word back to
Sparks to radio the Navy doctor for instructions.

A few minutes later the captain showed up with a radio message in his hand. "How's it going, Purser?"

"I think he's a goner."

"The Navy doctor says to give your patient a shot of adrenaline to the heart."

I balked at that. "He's *not my patient.*"

"He damned well is. You're ship's doctor."

"Only under your orders."

"Then I order you to give your patient a shot of adrenaline to
the heart."

"I wouldn't know how to do it. I might kill him."

"It's a direct order, Purser. Do it, or I'll throw you in the brig,
and bring you up on charges when we get back."

I looked around at my witnesses. "Put the order in writing,
Captain."

He found someone with pen and paper and wrote it out.

"Okay," I said, "but I'm sure he's dead already."

I got the adrenaline out of the medicine bag, found a hypo-
dermic and fresh needle, and prepared the injection. I looked up
at the captain one more time. "You sure?"

"If he's dead, there's nothing to lose."

"But I'm not sure."

"Do it!"

The men rolled him onto his back at my instruction.

With no heartbeat to guide me, I searched for where I hoped
this man's heart would be. I shoved the hypo in and jammed the
plunger.

Nothing.

The captain told the messenger to have Sparks notify the Navy doctor. Minutes later, the man returned with the message. The captain read it aloud. "Continue artificial respiration until midnight. Then declare the sailor dead."

"But he's dead already!"

"There's going to be a Naval inquest. Go ahead, Purse, follow the doctor's orders."

"Why me?"

"Because you're the duly appointed doctor on this ship, and he's your patient, and you've got your order in writing."

We rolled the dead seaman back onto his stomach, and for the next hour and a half, I sat astride a stiffening corpse, whispering, "Out goes the bad air. In comes the good."

At midnight, I declared him dead. After we wrapped him in canvas, I asked the captain if we would bury him at sea.

"Can't do it. We're two days off the Florida coast. I have to bring him in for the inquiry."

"Where do we keep him until then?"

The captain shrugged. "Put him into the refrigerator."

A murmur of disapproval at the captain's words traveled from the seamen at the entrance to the fo'c'sle, all the way back to the catwalk. The bosun stepped through the crowd, pushed the onlookers outside, and closed the hatch.

"Cap'n, with all respects . . ."

"What is it, Boats?"

"The men don't take to the idea of having a dead man stored in with their food. A lot of them are real superstitious. I think you'd have a mutiny on your hands."

The captain looked at me. "Any suggestions, *Doctor*?"

I winced at the word. "We've got him wrapped in waterproof canvas. Why don't we just put him on some boards in one of the empty cargo holds and pile dry ice around him?"

The bosun nodded. "That won't bother them."

"Okay, Boats," the captain said. "Have the deck crew take care of it." Then he turned on his heel and climbed the ladder to the catwalk and back to officers' quarters.

We anchored off Fort Lauderdale, and I watched from the railing as a launch brought Navy officers out to the *Polestar.* Although I had done the best I could under the captain's direct orders, I was frightened and nervous about the inquiry. I put his written orders into my briefcase and congratulated myself on my foresight. What would have happened to me without them? Might I have been accused of practicing medicine without a license? Manslaughter? Well, aboard ship, a captain was all-powerful. He had said I was a doctor, and that made it so.

It was a perfunctory inquiry. The ruling was something like "self-inflicted accidental death," and I was cleared.

After we arrived in port, my job was to assist the shipping commissioner who brought aboard ship's articles for the sign-off. I gave each man his official U.S. Coast Guard Certificate of Discharge.

But when the time came to sign ship's articles for the next voyage, only the officers signed on, none of the crew. As the bosun had said, most seamen were superstitious, and a ship aboard which a sailor had died was considered a vessel of doom. Despite my having been cleared at the inquest, they had all seen or heard how I had sat astride the dead man, and the word spread that I was a Jonah who urged him on with my incantation of good and bad air, squeezing the breath out of him, as I had ridden his soul down to hell.

Out on deck, I ran into the Bosun and some of the crew ready to go ashore. Feeling guilty under the stare of the dead man's shipmates, I said, "Sorry I couldn't save him."

The Bosun put his hand on my shoulder. "You did all you could, Purse. Most doctors lose a patient now and then."

As I watched them go down the gangway, his words hit home.

I'd kept my promise to my parents, and practiced medicine, but I'd lost a patient. I knew that when my eighteen months' tour of duty was over and I signed off the *Polestar*, that would end my medical career.

Like Somerset Maugham and Chekhov and Conan Doyle, I had been a doctor for a while, and like them I had failed. Now, I would keep following in their footsteps and try to become a writer.

PART TWO

||||||||||||||||||||||

From Ship to Shrink

6

||||||||||||||||||||||||

INKBLOTS

I SHIPPED OUT on the *Polestar* a second time, a planned one-year voyage from Newport News, Virginia, to Naples, and then a shuttle run carrying oil from Bahrain, Arabia, to the Naval station on Okinawa. However, the Navy changed our orders three times, and we ended up circling the globe in ninety-one days. When I signed off the *Polestar*, I said good-bye and good riddance to my seagoing medical career.

During six more voyages on other ships, I never once mentioned to any of the captains that I was first aid expert. Then, finally, after eighteen months of sea duty, I signed off my last oil tanker on December 6, 1946, with a Certificate of Continuous Service and a letter under presidential seal from the White House.

To you who answered the call of your country and served in its Merchant Marine to bring about the total defeat of the enemy, I extend the heartfelt thanks of the Nation. You undertook a most severe task—one which called for courage and fortitude. Because you demonstrated the resourcefulness

and calm judgment necessary to carry out that task, we now
look to you for leadership and example in further serving
our country in peace.

Signed: Harry Truman

I went back to my parents' home in Brooklyn where I planned
to live while I continued my college education.

My first day home after my discharge, Mom made a large dinner, and invited relatives and guests to celebrate my sister Gail's
ninth birthday and my return. The nineteen-year-old prodigal
son, my parents assumed, would now go on to become a doctor.
I hadn't yet gotten up the courage to tell them I had already fulfilled my promise by practicing medicine aboard ship, and I had
no intention of continuing premed or going to medical school.

After dinner, I headed down to my cellar library for a novel to
read in bed. But as I opened the door—even before I took the
stairs down—I sensed something was missing. Where was the
smell of wet coal?

I turned on the light and saw that my bookshelves, books and
all, were gone. I tasted panic in my throat as I walked quickly to
the alcove behind the steps. The coal bin was gone, and the old
furnace had been replaced by an oil-burner.

No books. No coal. No toys in the bin. All the real things were
gone. I wanted to dash upstairs and ask my parents, "Why?"

But it wasn't necessary. I understood. They had decided I was
no longer a child. I had left as a seventeen-year-old surrogate to
their dreams and they had gotten rid of my childish things. They
could never have known that their son's ideas and memories and
dreams—things he would use to make himself a writer—would
always occupy the hideaway beneath the cellar steps.

At breakfast next morning, I told them I had already tasted a
doctor's life, and like Maugham and Chekhov and Doyle, I had

failed at it. I was not cut out to practice medicine. I was going to become a writer, I said, and now I had to leave Brooklyn to do it.

My mother wept and my father walked out of the room.

I moved from my parents' apartment to an inexpensive furnished room on the west side of Manhattan, in the neighborhood called Hell's Kitchen. What money I had left from my service pay would have to support me while I wrote my first novel. It was about a seventeen-year-old purser's adventures at sea.

The novel was rejected by a dozen publishers. The last one had left a reader's coverage behind in the manuscript. By mistake? On purpose? Only two lines remain in my memory. The critique began: "It isn't as bad as some unsolicited manuscripts, but it's not good enough..." And the last line: "The basic story is good, but it is all on the surface and the characters' motivations are never too clear."

Like most writers, I took solace in the opening and closing phrases, putting the two *but*s out of my mind.

I reread the novel and saw how amateurish it was, how much I had to learn before I could call myself an author: how to get beneath the surface, how to understand a character's motivation, how to revise. I put the manuscript aside, knowing I would have to find another profession to support myself while I learned how to write.

Many writers began as reporters, among them Twain, Hemingway, and Stephen Crane. Well, why not?

A few days after my novel was rejected, I went to the *New York Times* building in Times Square, and asked to speak to the publisher. Only now do I realize how presumptuous it was of me to approach Mr. Ochs without an appointment or introduction, how amazing it was that I actually got in to see him, and how generous it was of him to give me the time.

"I'd like to start as a cub reporter," I told him, "then to become a foreign correspondent."

"Has that always been your goal?"

I squirmed as I searched for the right words. "Well, not exactly. My real goal is to be an author."

He nodded gravely and turned a framed picture on his desk to show me a photograph of a young man. "I'm going to tell you the same thing I told my son," he said. "In the immortal words of the famous journalist and author Horace Greeley, 'Go west, young man. Go west.'"

I suspected that Mr. Ochs interpreted Greeley as advising young would-be authors and journalists to hone their skills and seek their opportunities away from New York, somewhere in the minor leagues.

I thanked him for his advice, but I didn't follow it. Instead, I enrolled in a summer-session journalism course at NYU. I sat in a crowded lecture hall for two weeks before I realized that I would have to devote all my time, energy, and single-minded striving to become a good reporter. Using words constantly in newspaper work, I realized, would leave me too tired to create fiction at night. I dropped the course, got back part of my tuition, and searched for another career that wouldn't interfere with writing.

I applied to Brooklyn College, which, at that time, was free for those whose high school records showed a B average, or who achieved a B or higher in an admissions examination. Unfortunately, I had been a C+ student. In high school, my English teachers had always given me A for creativity and D for grammar and usage. But I placed high on the entrance exam, was accepted for tuition-free admission, and resumed my college education at night.

I was still trying to decide what profession might leave me energy and time to write. I enrolled in an introductory psychology course and found the subject matter fascinating, the instructor stimulating. I was surprised to learn that he was a lay psychoanalyst—not a psychiatrist with an M.D.—and that with only a Master of Arts degree he had developed a clinical practice.

Here, I decided, was my solution.

As a lay psychoanalyst, I would be able to set my own hours for therapy sessions and charge reasonable fees for helping people deal with their mental problems. I would learn about peoples' motives, and come to understand their conflicts. And I imagined how that would help me create believable characters—living, suffering, changing characters—for my stories and novels.

As Faulkner said in 1950 when he accepted the Nobel Prize for Literature: "... the young man or woman writing today has forgotten the problems of the human heart in conflict with itself which alone can make good writing because only that is worth writing about, worth the agony and the sweat... leaving no room in his workshop for anything but the old verities and truths of the heart, the old universal truths lacking which any story is ephemeral and doomed..."

Instead of exploring "the human heart in conflict with itself," I decided I would write about the *human mind* in conflict with itself, and psychology would be my path. I declared it my major.

I took a daytime job selling encyclopedias from door to door. I hated the cold-calling, high-pressure selling, but I was good at it and the commissions stopped the hemorrhaging from my savings account.

During this time, I took psychology, sociology, and anthropology courses, but the more courses I took, the more disillusioned I became. Not about the subject matter, but with the professors. Except for that first instructor who had inspired me, I found most of them dull, pedantic, and pompous, and their research trivial.

In my senior year, I confided some personal anxieties to my advisor, a professor of Psychological Tests and Measurements. She gave me the Rorschach test, and as I responded to the inkblots, a memory flooded my mind.

... I see a little first or second grader sitting at the kitchen table doing his homework, dipping a steel-nibbed pen into a bottle of black ink, and scratching cursive letters in a black-and-white-marble covered notebook. As he nears the end of the page, the boy's hand trembles. He presses too hard on the pen. A blob of ink flows down the nib, and before he can lift it from the page, an inkblot drips onto the paper.

He knows what will happen. For the third time that evening—after two errors and now one inkblot—a hand comes out of the shadows, over his shoulder, and rips the page from the notebook.

"Do it over," his mother says. "It has to be perfect."

After the Rorschach, my advisor, the professor of Tests and Measurements refused to discuss the results, and never spoke to me again. I thought of going to another Rorschach specialist to find out what those inkblots had revealed, but I decided I was better off not knowing.

Years later, I satirized some of my psych professors in "Flowers for Algernon." Digging up that old homework inkblot memory, and my mother's hand tearing out the pages, I transformed my frustrating Tests and Measurements advisor into Burt the tester whom Charlie Gordon frustrates with his responses to the inkblots.

Writers get even.

7

||||||||||||||||||||||||||

THE BOY ON BOOK MOUNTAIN

AFTER GRADUATING *summa cum ordinary* in 1950, I took a one-year postgraduate course at CCNY, City College of New York. The course, called The Organismic Approach to Psychopathology, was given by the world-famous psychiatrist Kurt Goldstein. His method of teaching, both semesters, was to read to us—word for word, with an impenetrable German accent—his book: *The Organismic Approach to Psychopathology.*

During the same period, I began what was called a *didactic analysis.* Anyone who hoped to practice pure psychoanalysis was expected to plumb his or her own depths, to unearth biases, traumas, and personality defects, and to be able to compensate for them when treating clients. I went twice a week, Mondays and Fridays, at the reduced rate of ten dollars for each fifty-minute hour.

My analyst was short, middle-aged, with a thick Austrian accent difficult to understand. He used the Freudian method—me stretched out on the couch, him sitting in a chair behind me, out of sight.

He laid down the ground rules, which I thought of as the Four Commandments. During the course of my analysis, I was to avoid making any major alterations in my life: I was not to change jobs,

move, get married or divorced, or—and this was especially important—I was not to quit therapy. These restrictions, he explained,
were based on the theory that painful self-awareness surfacing during depth therapy, along with transference with the analyst, often
leads people to find creative ways of dumping their therapists.
And therapists have reasons for not wanting that to happen.

I accepted the rules. Actually, I felt I'd be getting my money's
worth. In addition to becoming trained as a psychoanalyst, I'd be
getting an insight into myself and—at the same time—I'd learn
how to use the process of free association as a writing tool.

Three goals for the price of one was a bargain, but at first it
didn't work.

Although the dynamics of psychoanalysis require the analyst
to sit passively, and merely facilitate free association, I became
frustrated. Each time I lay on the couch, the first five or ten minutes of the fifty-minute hour came up blank or with inconse-
quential talk about what was currently going on in my life. One
afternoon, I sat up and faced him.

He looked startled.

"I seem to be wasting your time and my money," I said.

He cleared his throat to prepare it for the unorthodox proce-
dure of actually *talking to a client*. "Daniel, let me to you something explain. Is perfectly usual what you are experiencing. You
see, in Vienna, the analysand to therapy comes six days a week.
Only on Sundays are there no sessions. Is common experience that
after a day with no free association, the psychic wound a protective
layer forms, and on Monday, it takes a great deal of work to break
through to real, substantial association. This blankness, or garbage,
you experiencing are, we call, the *Monday Morning Crust*."

"I don't understand."

"Since you only twice a week to sessions come, with off-days
in between, it always some time takes to break through the *Monday Morning Crust*."

Although it seemed wasteful to spend ten minutes of each fifty-minute hour in silence or spewing out expensive emotional garbage before penetrating my mental crust, I lay back on the couch again. After ten minutes I began really free-associating. And I remembered...

...Betty's Beauty Parlor, near the railroad depot of freight sidings, beneath the elevated trains...my mother Betty, a self-trained beautician, washing, curling, and setting women's hair...

We live in one room above the beauty parlor, my bed beside the window close to theirs, and I wake up every time the elevated train thunders by...

...circus season...Ringling Brothers Barnum and Bailey Circus trains have pulled into the nearby freight yards. Side-show people and lady performers come to Betty's Beauty Parlor to have their hair and nails done. Some of them wait out on the stone porch, sitting on the steps, playing with me, doing tricks and telling stories. The bearded lady and the tattooed lady are my mother's customers. They say I am a cute little boy.

A lady trapeze artist comes to have her hair done. Her little girl...about five or six with blond Shirley Temple curls is crying as her mother drags her inside kicking and screaming.

My mother calls out to me to let the little girl play with my toys. I hand her a train engine from my toy box, but she flings it and it breaks.

"Danny," my mother says, "play with her."

No matter what I do the brat keeps crying.

"Danny..." my mother pleads.

I run upstairs and come back with an armload of my books. I open one and begin: "Once upon a time, there was a beautiful princess..."

Though the girl keeps crying, I don't stop. Eventually, she grows silent and listens. Of course, I can't really read at that age, but my mother has read the stories to me so often that I know them by heart.

"He can read!" one of the customers says.

The girl's mother asks, "How old is he?"

"Three and a half," my mother says proudly.

"He must be a genius." She opens her purse and takes out a penny. "That was very clever, Danny. Here, buy a piece of candy."

I tilt back my head and try to see my analyst's face. "I guess that's when I first learned I could be paid for telling stories."

I can't make out his face, and he makes no comment.

I must have been three or four years old when those memories were locked in, because Wall Street collapsed in 1929 when I was two, and President Roosevelt closed the banks in 1933 when I was five. Some time between those two dates, my parents were forced to close Betty's Beauty Parlor and move to Snediker Avenue, where they rented two first-floor rooms from Mr. Pincus.

When the hard times came, since my mother had no time to read me to sleep, I taught myself the alphabet. Sounding out the words came easily, and I was a reader long before I entered first grade at the age of six. The teachers at P.S. 63 convinced my mother that there was no point in sending a five-year-old who could read as well as I did to kindergarten.

I associate the connections of memory to the age of six or seven when I first learned what it meant to be a storyteller.

On a humid summer evening, as my parents and I sat on the front porch, I discovered a group of neighborhood kids congregated under the streetlamp in front of the local grocery store.

With my mother's permission, I ran to see what was going on.

Most of the boys were older, and they were in front of the store sitting on large wooden crates the grocer used to keep milk bottles cold in the wintertime. Someone boosted me up to sit with them so I could watch and hear.

A boy named Sammy stood on the sidewalk telling a story. I still see him clearly, his uncut hair falling over his ears, his shirt patched, his scuffed black shoes unlaced.

He told of Joan of Arc being attacked by the Frankenstein monster, saved in the nick of time by the Hunchback of Notre Dame. And then King Kong captured Mae West and dragged her out into the jungle, but Charlie Chaplin had a sword in his cane, and he killed the huge ape and wandered off twirling his cane.

Everyone sitting on the wooden boxes listened intently as Sammy unfolded his tales. They screamed with disappointment when he stopped with the hated words: "To be continued..."

Tony, the next storyteller, tried to imitate Sammy, but he didn't have it. He rambled and lost track of his plots, and the audience showed their disapproval by banging their heels on the sides of the empty milk boxes.

In the summer evenings that followed, I was always there to listen, and to learn what kinds of stories made them kick, and what kept them silent. I wanted to join in, to show that I, too, could be a storyteller, but at six or seven I was the youngest and too frightened to perform in front of this audience of tough critics.

I couldn't seem to memorize anything. At home, before joining the group in front of the grocery store, I planned my plots and visualized how I would tell the stories. But when it was my turn, I became confused.

It was the same at school. I did poorly on tests that relied on memory. My mother would get me up early in the morning before a math test to review the multiplication tables, but by the time I got to class it was all gone.

Years earlier, I'd been able to memorize stories from children's books word for word, without even trying, but later, in school, I couldn't recall anything. I guessed I wasn't very bright.

Then one night, in bed, with my eyes closed, I tried to review for the next day's arithmetic test, going over the material again and again. Nothing. Forcing myself to stay awake, I tried to see the numbers. I couldn't add or subtract without counting on my fingers. But next morning, while washing my face with icy water, I stared into the mirror over the sink, eyes stinging with soap. I knew that I knew it all. I rattled off the eight and nine times tables to my reflection.

Between night and morning, no matter how hard I'd struggled, after failing to get this stuff straight in my head, something or someone *had learned it in my sleep.*

I applied the system to the grocery storytelling group: struggle with the material hard before sleep, then put it out of my mind. In the morning I face the other me in the mirror, and discover I've got it.

It took me a long time to get up the nerve to perform, but with sleep learning, I had my stories down cold. My plots were dramatic, filled with menace and conflict, and my audience never banged their heels against the boxes.

Years later, I published a short story about Sammy—called "The Spellbinder"—in the *North American Review.* And I transformed my memory of learning during sleep into the sleep-learning machine that Charlie Gordon struggles with during the experiment to increase his intelligence and knowledge.

"I loved storytelling almost as much as I loved books," I told my analyst.

"And what does that make you think of?" he asked in one of his more talkative moments.

"It reminds me of climbing Book Mountain..."

"Yes...?"

I remembered.

By the time I was in third grade, my father had worked out a partnership deal with a potbellied, bald man whose name I don't remember. They opened a junk shop in Brownsville and bought and sold scrap metal, old clothing, and newspapers. Junkmen would pull up to the warehouse with horses and wagons and unload their day's accumulation onto the huge scale.

From time to time, my father would take me with him and let me play in the shop. What interested me most was the mountain of books...

...It's a hot August day, the summer I turn eight.... My father explains that he and his partner pay a few cents for boxes of old books to be baled, and pulped into cheap paper. "You can take some books home."

"To keep?"

"Sure."

"How many?"

He hands me a small burlap sack. "As many as you can carry."

I can still visualize the books piled up to the ceiling. I see three huge men, stripped to the waist, bodies glistening with sweat, bandanas around their foreheads, loading books into a baling press.

One worker grabs an armful from the base of the huge pile, rips off the covers, and hands the naked pages to a second worker who dumps them into the baler. The third tamps them down and sets the baler's press lid.

Then the first man punches the button that crushes the books, and I hear the grinding sound. The second man inserts wires into the machine that will make wire-bound bales encased in cardboard from old boxes. The third man opens the machine and pulls the bale out with a hand truck and deposits it on the street with the others so the truck will be able to back up, load them, and drive them away to pulp them into rolls of paper.

Suddenly, I know what I have to do. I climb up to the top of Book Mountain and make a place to sit. I grab a book, read a few passages, and either toss it down to the base or put it into my bag. Quickly, I go through as many as I can, desperately sampling enough of a book to decide if it's worth rescuing from the sweating book destroyers who will feed them to the baler below.

When I've got six or seven books, I slide down the other side of the mountain and load the sack into my bicycle basket.

At home most evenings, when schoolwork is done, instead of listening to the radio serials, I read, and read, and read. Many of the books are too advanced for me, but I know that someday I will understand them. Someday I will learn what they have to teach.

The image of myself as a boy going up and then coming down Book Mountain is fixed in my memory as the icon of my love of reading and learning.

It was clear to me as I wrote "Flowers for Algernon" where the shape of it came from. As Charlie's intelligence increases, I visualize him ascending a mountain. The higher he climbs, the farther he sees, until at the peak, he turns and sees all around him the world of knowledge—of good and evil.

But then he must come down the other side.

8

||||||||||||||||||||||||

SILENCE OF THE
PSYCHOANALYSTS

MY PSYCHOANALYST'S LACK of any kind of response began to oppress me, and I found myself wondering about him. Like that Tests and Measurements advisor who avoided me after the inkblot test, this shrink never talked to me either!

Without confiding in him, I quit selling encyclopedias from door to door and found a new job at Acme Advertising selling direct-mail advertising—mailers with attached return order envelopes. The company called us *Account Executives,* but it was still cold-calling—just one notch above ringing doorbells.

When I told my analyst that I had violated his first commandment against making changes in my life, he said nothing.

During my first *executive* meeting at Acme Advertising, I met Bergie, a tall, heavyset man who knew the good local restaurants and enjoyed talking about books. When he referred to the company as *Acne* instead of *Acme,* I knew I had found a friend.

One day, he asked me to join him for a brown-bag lunch at the Peter Fland Photographic Studio between Broadway and Sixth Avenue—a block from the Forty-second Street Library. He and two Austrian friends, who worked at Fland's as retouchers of photographic negatives, had formed a chamber music trio, and they played in the studio after their lunch break.

Fland was a jolly, bouncing photographer, with an Austrian accent, whose every comment conveyed good-natured irony. The luncheon concert was followed by a photo shoot, and he invited me to watch. Three tall fashion models came in and lounged about, waiting, looking bored, almost glum. The red-head sipped coffee out of a paper cup, the brunette chain-smoked cigarettes, the third, a blond, was filing her fingernails.

A few minutes later, a short, dark-haired young woman entered the studio. Her boss was studying a still-wet 8 × 10 black-and-white print.

"Ahh, Aurea!" he said. "You were right about the backlight!"

Aurea rearranged the lighting, then slipped out of her shoes to step onto the set and called the models back. She styled the dresses, pulling the brunette's out to flare. When the blond's dress wouldn't stay put, Aurea took a spool of fine thread out of her pocket, pinned one thread to each side of the hem, pulled them out, and pinned the other ends of the threads to the floor. The redhead's dress was too tight, so Aurea slit it down the back, and arranged the front folds to drape naturally. Then she stepped aside.

"Perfect!" Fland shouted. "Lights!"

She threw the switches.

The instant the set was illuminated by floodlights the models were transformed. Wet lips glistened, eyes opened wide. They came alive, exciting and alluring under the lights, as Fland took dozens of shots.

"Okay!" he called out. "That's beautiful, ladies."

The moment Aurea switched off the lights, the three models drooped like puppets whose strings had been released. They were bored again, glum, almost plain.

I nodded. Few things were what they appeared to be.

I stopped by the Fland Studio often, before my evening graduate psych courses at CCNY, trying to work up the nerve to invite Aurea out to dinner, or to the theater—for the full three acts, of course.

One Friday afternoon, I got a call from a writer-acquaintance named Lester del Rey. He wanted to know if I was interested in a job as associate fiction editor for a chain of pulps. These were the popular fiction magazines of the day, printed on cheap, untrimmed stock that left paper dandruff all over your dark clothing.

"I don't understand," I said.

"Well, my agent, Scott Meredith, has heard of an opening at Stadium Publications. He's close to the editor, and Scott would like to have the job filled by someone who'd buy stories from Meredith clients. I told him that even though you haven't published yet, you've got a good story sense, and might be able to handle the job. It pays fifty dollars a week. Interested?"

Thinking I'd be violating my analyst's First Commandment about not changing jobs a second time, I hesitated, but I said yes.

"Okay, come down to Scott's office. By the time you get here, he'll have a letter of recommendation typed up, and he'll call ahead and set up a meeting between you and Bob Erisman."

"How can Meredith recommend me? He's never met me."

Lester paused. "Don't ask any questions. If you want the job, just get over here quick."

By the time I arrived at the Scott Meredith Literary Agency, Lester had left, but fast-talking Meredith filled me in on the situation.

"Bob Erisman works at his home in Connecticut, and comes into New York only on Fridays to pick up the edited stories. His associate fiction editor quit without notice, and he's desperate for a replacement."

He handed me a note: "From the desk of SCOTT MERED-ITH—September 1, 1950." It introduced me as an excellent candidate for the position. It said I'd worked at his literary agency for about six months on a temporary job, and had experience doing pulp reading for another periodical. They'd sold a few of my baseball, football, and science fiction stories.

I swallowed hard. We'd never get away with this.

His note praised me as a fast reader and typist, familiar with general magazine practice. The quoted salary, he wrote, was acceptable.

When I said nothing, Meredith asked what I thought of the letter.

I shrugged. "The last line is true."

"Good," he said. "Then you'd better get over there before Bob leaves for the week."

Martin Goodman Publications, and its pulp magazine subsidiary, Stadium Publications, were on the sixteenth floor of the Empire State Building. I got there at three o'clock, and Bob Erisman, the editor, was waiting for me.

He got up from behind his desk to greet me, took the letter of recommendation, and nodded as he read it. "Good. Scott Meredith is a great judge of people. You start a two-week trial period on Monday."

He led me to the adjoining office that held two desks. At the one near the window, a portly, old gentleman with horn-rimmed glasses halfway down his nose, was puffing away at a pipe clenched between his teeth.

"This is the editor of our true crime and fact detective lines," Erisman said, introducing us. "Daniel Keyes is trying out for the associate fiction editor's job."

The old gentleman peered at me over his glasses, saluted with his blue pencil, grunted his approval, and went back to editing through his pipe smoke.

Erisman led me to a smaller desk against the other wall and pointed to different colored binders stacked on shelves. "Those are the agents' submissions. Dirk Wylie Agency, Lenninger Agency, Matson, and so forth. As you know, the gray ones are from Scott."

I nodded, starting to sweat.

He pointed to a garish red and yellow magazine cover on the wall. The May issue of *Best Western* highlighted a damsel in distress held hostage by a mean-faced, unshaven cowpoke, while the hero's white horse reared as a rifle shot exploded across the yellow background. The blurb read: "WHERE THE GUNHAWKS GATHER, A filed .45 was the kid's only friend in vengeance valley...Smash feature-length novel." Near the top, a banner heading read, 3 BRAND NEW NOVELS PLUS SHORT STORIES.

Erisman said, "You'll go through the agents' manuscripts and select and edit the stories to go with the novels."

I picked up the slender magazine. "Three novels?"

He shrugged. "They're really long stories, or short novelettes, but readers like to think they're getting their twenty-five cents' worth."

"I don't select those?"

"Novels are commissioned from our top writers in each field, and I edit them. I also write the blurbs, the titles, and describe the drawings for the artists. You buy and edit the short stories. We have nine monthly magazines. Four westerns, four sports, and one science fiction. Why don't you take a few of each and get a feeling for the kind of material our readers like."

He looked at his watch. "I've got to catch my train. See you next Friday. Before you leave, drop in at the business office, and they'll put you on the payroll."

After he was gone, I sat down at my new desk and tried out the swivel chair. The true crime editor was too deep in his work to notice me. I picked up copies of *Complete Sports, Complete Westerns, Western Novels and Stories,* and *Marvel Science Fiction.*

"So long," I said to my office mate. "Nice meeting you. Have a good weekend."

He waved his blue pencil at me without looking up.

I glanced around the offices on my way out. I was actually going to be paid a regular weekly salary of fifty dollars to read, buy, and edit stories. I had landed on the first step of a career that would support me while I wrote fiction. Then I was through the door, down the elevator, and out onto Fifth Avenue to catch the bus that would take me to my psychoanalyst's office. I was apprehensive. I had violated the first of his Four Commandments twice in a matter of months.

I got there a few minutes early, and as I waited I flipped through *Complete Westerns.* Almost immediately, I saw two typographical errors. That's when I realized that, despite Scott Meredith's recommendation attesting to my familiarity with general magazine practice, I didn't know the first thing about *editing* a manuscript.

As I held the magazine, my hands trembled, and I started to sweat. Something was coming into my mind. Something deep and frightening. The memory of my mother's hand ripping out my homework page. Her words, echoing... "It has to be perfect."

When I finally got on the couch, I said, "I've got a new job. I'm quitting Acme Advertising. I'm going to edit a chain of pulp magazines."

I expected him to say something like: Oh, you've quit another job? But he didn't respond.

I said, "I must admit I feel guilty at breaking one of the rules you laid down—not once but twice—but I hate cold-call selling, and I'm excited about climbing the first rung up the literary ladder."

After fifty minutes, filled with long periods of silence, I got off the couch, paid him, and left. As much as his lack of response irritated me, I realized his method was working. There in his consulting room, I had just associated my new editing job with the earlier inkblot memory of my mother's demand for writing perfection.

Although I felt confident about finding and correcting mistakes, editing paragraphs and sentences, and fixing errors, I suddenly wondered, what about editorial notations and proofreaders' marks?

Well, I thought, mumbling the cliché that has served me all my life, "Where there's a will there's a way." Instead of going to my room, I took a Fifth Avenue bus to the Forty-second Street Library to read up on editing and proofreading marks.

No movies, or ball games, or working up the nerve to ask Aurea for a date—not for a while. Erisman would come into the office next Friday to pick up the stories. I had just one week to learn to be an editor.

9

||||||||||||||||||||||||

FIRST PUBLISHED STORIES

MY FIRST WEEK AT STADIUM PUBLICATIONS went well. I read through agents' submissions in each category, and out of loyalty and gratitude, I read those from Scott Meredith first. Unfortunately, his western and sports writers left me cold. I selected one from another agency, and then I glanced through the unsolicited manuscripts, sometimes called "over the transom," or the "slush pile," and chose one I liked.

I found editing easier than I'd expected. I trimmed wordy sentences, toned down purple prose, removed redundancies, and deleted clichés.

Erisman picked the stories up on Friday and said he'd let me know before the end of the following week if the job was mine. It was a long, agonizing weekend, but the following Tuesday, he phoned me from his home in Connecticut to tell me I was hired.

The following week, I learned of a Manhattan apartment that was about to become available. It was next door to Lester del Rey, who had recommended me to Scott Meredith. The rent-controlled cold-water flat on West End Avenue and Sixty-sixth Street had been leased to Philip Klass, the brother of my Merchant Marine friend, Morton Klass. Phil, who wrote humorous science fiction under the pen name William Tenn, had just found a larger place. I rented the apartment.

When I told my analyst that I had just violated his Second Commandment—"Thou shalt not move during therapy"—he made no comment. But a sigh of disapproval hung over the couch.

"This was one deal I couldn't pass up," I said.

Nothing.

I reassured myself that he'd get over it. Although it was a Friday, I had a thick and chewy Monday Morning Crust.

The apartment. What can I say about it? My rent, after a 15 percent increase, would be $17.25 per month. (That is not a typographical error.) The front door opened to a very long, dark corridor leading to a kitchen heated by a kerosene stove. To the left of the refrigerator, the bathtub was concealed by a hinged lid. Although a bathtub in the kitchen seemed odd, now I realized it made sense to bathe in the warmest room in the apartment.

It also clarified something that had long baffled me.

Thomas Wolfe, who had taught creative writing at NYU in the '30s, had later been described by his biographers as writing longhand, using the top of his refrigerator as a desk, and throwing page after page into his bathtub.

I'd read that Wolfe had been a giant of a man, but I was confused by the picture of him tossing finished pages into the bathtub. I couldn't visualize the action. Did he run back and forth from kitchen to bathroom after each page?

Now I understood. He must have lived in a flat like this, with the bathtub alongside the refrigerator. And I could visualize him writing furiously, flipping page after page into the tub, then scooping them out, packing and delivering them to Maxwell

Perkins at Scribners, who would organize, edit, and shape them into *Look Homeward, Angel.*

Oh, for editors like that today.

Oh, for *apartments* like that today! I still dream of it.

Unlike Thomas Wolfe, I am far too short to use the top of the refrigerator as a desk, and, besides, in those days I used an old Royal typewriter. On cold days, I worked sitting down in the adjacent room, wearing a heavy sweater and a knit cap, using an overturned wooden crate as a typewriter table.

I set aside my notes for a rewrite of my sea novel and began my first serious attempts to write short fiction for the magazines.

The hour is late, and though I'm tired, I want to keep going, to get all this down. But Hemingway taught us in his posthumous memoir, *A Moveable Feast,* that it's necessary, after you achieved something and know what's going to happen next, to stop and put it *out* of your mind—which really means put it *into* your unconscious—and let it work. I've always suspected he learned that from Mark Twain who said it was necessary to leave the writing pump primed so it would start up easily when you began again the next day.

I had developed another image for the difficulty of getting started writing after missing even a single day. It was like the Monday Morning Crust of psychoanalysis. Just as the mental scab over the psychic wound had to be broken before free association could flow again, so for the writer the creative wound crusted as well. To avoid risking writer's block, I write every morning, seven days a week, if I can.

Any day I'm unable to write, because I'm traveling or attending to urgent matters, I feel miserable. But when I'm able to break through and pick up from where I left off the day before, the writing feels glorious.

———

My first published short story appeared in one of my own western magazines, under a pseudonym that I will not reveal even under threat of torture. Here's how it happened.

A few months after I started work, the advertising department phoned. Some clients had pulled ads from the next issue of *Western Stories,* and I would need to fill the space with 3,000 words of fiction. I searched through the agents' folders. No 3,000-word westerns.

I turned to the bundles of unsolicited manuscripts in the slush pile. Most of the stories were too long. The few that looked short didn't indicate a word count, and of course I didn't have time to count them. That's when I learned the importance of always including a word count in the upper right-hand corner of the first page, below the words "First Serial Rights Only."

I swiveled in my chair. Since I couldn't find a story of the needed length, there was only one thing left for me to do. The magazine needed a story to fill the gap. It was an emergency. And, after all, I selected the stories. Why not write the story myself? Not for the money, mind you—at a penny a word, less an agent's 10 percent commission, it would come to twenty-four bucks—but to solve the space problem. And, besides, to see my words in print for the first time.

Of course, I would have to use a pen name and submit the story through one of the regular agents. I phoned one and explained the situation. It was very common, he said, and agreed to represent me.

That night, after dinner, I sat down to write. First, a western-sounding title. Remembering that one of my ships had loaded oil in the Texas gulf port of Aransas Pass, I typed: "BUSHWHACK AT ARANSAS PASS." Three thousand words would be a breeze.

On Friday, Erisman brought back the previous week's stories, again complimented me on my judgment, and picked up the new batch. But the following week he said, "Another great lineup,

Dan, except for that 3,000-word 'Aransas Pass' thing. What a terrible story! What awful writing! I can't imagine what possessed you to buy it."

I swallowed hard. "Well, it was an emergency, and it was the only 3,000-word filler I could find. I see some talent in this guy. I thought I'd encourage him."

Erisman frowned and looked at me hard. "Well, maybe."

"What didn't you like about it?"

"Oh, come on, Dan. He doesn't miss a western cliché. Every character is a stereotype. The plot is corny. Some glimmer of writing talent, I agree, but he's got a lot to learn."

"I was hoping to bring him along."

He pursed his lips, held my gaze with his soft blue eyes, and shrugged. "Well, maybe. But he's got to edit his work. I know most of our B-list writers are getting paid a cent a word, but that's for lean copy, not padding. Tell him that good, tight writing comes from shaking each page and letting any word, or sentence, fall out if it won't be missed."

"Hemingway's style," I said.

"Exactly. Hem once said that if you didn't know something, it left a hole in your work. But if you knew it and deleted it, the work would be stronger."

"So that's how he did it, by shaking out the excess."

Erisman nodded, dropped the *Western Stories* manuscripts on my desk, and picked up my edited stack of manuscripts for *Best Sports Stories.*

"Too bad Hemingway didn't do sports stories," I said.

"Didn't he?" Erisman's eyebrows went up. "Tell your young writer to read 'My Old Man,' about horse racing, and 'The Short Happy Life of Francis Macomber,' about lion hunting, and 'Fifty Grand,' about boxing, and one of the really great novels, *The Sun Also Rises,* about bullfighting, with the incredible scene of running the bulls in Pamplona, and about deep-sea fishing in *The Old Man and the Sea.*"

"Oh, well, I didn't think of those as—"

"As commercial fiction? Dan, we're talking about style. And for the purest style that got him the Nobel Prize for Literature, read—I mean, *tell your young writer to read*—"The Killers" and "A Clean, Well-Lighted Place.""

"I-I'll tell him."

"Can't stay today," he said. "I'm looking forward to seeing the *Marvel Science Fiction* lineup next week. We'll have lunch at Childs."

After he left, I sat back in my chair, took a few deep breaths, and went through a pile of science fiction stories with gray folders from the shelves behind me. One was by Lester del Rey.

Since he had helped me get this job, I read his story eagerly. The plot was original, the scenes absorbing, but oddly enough, it seemed wordy. To use Erisman's phrase, the pages needed shaking out.

I called Scott and told him how much I liked the story, but that I thought it needed minor revisions.

There was a silence at the other end, and then, with slow, deadly emphasis, he said, "*Lester...doesn't...rewrite.* He gets *two* cents a word. If he revises his work that would mean he's getting only *one* cent a word."

"I see."

"Are you going to buy it?"

I took a deep breath. It was presumptuous of me but I couldn't compromise what I felt strongly. "Not as it is, Scott. Sorry."

"That's all right, Dan. I wanted to give you first shot at a new del Rey story. I'll sell it to another magazine without any trouble."

He did.

By this time, I thought I should get a regular literary agent, so

I delivered three early pieces of work to Scott Meredith for consideration. His two-and-a-half-page letter shows how naive I was. He, or more likely one of his readers, wrote that my writing showed promise but the stories "were off the beam for marketing."

There followed a reasonable analysis of the three pieces, none of which were ever published because they are indeed amateurish, apprentice work. He was not sending me an agent's contract, Meredith said, because he didn't feel that either of us should be tied down at this point.

I wrote a new story called "Something Borrowed," and submitted it to another agent who specialized in science fiction. Frederik Pohl, at the Dirk Wylie Literary Agency, wrote me his impressions.

The trouble with the piece, he explained, was that it was a Ray Bradbury–type story, and that nobody but Bradbury ought to write Bradbury stories.

Then he softened the blow by adding that he expected to sell "Something Borrowed." He felt I could do much better, he said, and was eagerly awaiting my next story.

That night, as I flipped through my idea folders, I saw a scrawled note, *"What would happen if we could increase human intelligence artificially?"* I remembered wondering about that many years earlier as I had waited for the train that would take me to class at NYU.

Turning a few more pages, I saw the title, "Guinea Pig," followed with just a couple of typed lines:

Story similar to "The Man Who Could Work Miracles." Plain guy becomes a genius by brain surgery—experiences fantastic heights.

The word *surgery* flashed me back to my biology class dissection. It hadn't been a guinea pig, I thought, but a white mouse!

But the man *would* be used as a guinea pig. I realized this memory, drawn out of the depths of my mind, was turning into an idea for a story. But that's all it was—an idea.

It didn't occur to me then that mulling over the concept of making someone a genius through brain surgery was the first step on my journey to find a character that both I and the reader could care about.

The mouse didn't become Algernon until much later.

10

||||||||||||||||||||||

Editing Pulps and Writing Comic Books

Aurea and I began dating regularly. Although we fell in love, we agreed that before we could think of marriage I would have to be solidly on the path to becoming a professional writer.

In 1950 and 1951 I wrote more westerns for our magazines under pseudonyms, and Erisman agreed that the young writer I had taken under my wing when I bought his first western story had come along nicely. "His style has improved: no more clichés, tighter prose, cleaner plot. He spins a good yarn. There's even a hint of characterization."

But I still hadn't published anything under my own name.

In the spring of 1952 I was asked by the editor of *Other Worlds Science Stories* to submit a story for a special "All Star Editor Issue!" It was going to feature six stories by science fiction editors. If they bought my story, I would be paid two cents a word.

I thought of the "Guinea Pig" idea, about increasing human intelligence through surgery, but I sensed it would be a complex story. I didn't feel ready to write it, so I put it out of my mind and kept searching.

I found another idea in my note folder. What if a slave-robot was emancipated? How would it deal with antirobot prejudice? How would he support himself?

In the same folder, I saw a note. *"Algernon Charles Swinburne. Odd first name."* Maybe I would name the first free robot Algernon. I decided, instead, to name the robot—Robert.

I mentioned the emancipated robot concept to Lester del Rey over coffee, and he offered me fifty dollars for the idea. It was tempting, but I figured if Lester was willing to buy it, it must be worth writing.

"Robot Unwanted," my first real publication under my own name, was the lead story in the issue. It was 5,000 words long, and the check, after a 10 percent deduction for the agent's fee, was for $90.

The one copy I still have is on crumbling pulp paper, and as I open to it the page comes loose. The blurb reads: *"Robert was the only one on Earth—an F.R. That meant he was a free robot; free to do anything he wanted—but he didn't want to die!"*

For a writer, there is no feeling to match the elation that comes from seeing your name in print under the title of your first published work. As you walk the streets of Manhattan, you wonder why people aren't rushing up to ask for your autograph. You toy with the idea of quitting your job and writing full-time for fame and fortune.

When the rejections of other stories keep coming, you drift back down to earth.

But some people in the closely knit science fiction writing and publishing community took note. Many SF editors, agents, and writers had known each other as fans in the early years. One such group called itself the Hydra Club. I had met many of its members and was often invited to their parties, but I was too young to be accepted into this circle.

One Friday afternoon, after the publication of "Robot Unwanted," I got a phone call, inviting me to join a poker game at the home of H. L. Gold, which was also the office of *Galaxy*, the magazine he edited. I'd heard stories that since his return from World War II duty, Horace had developed agoraphobia, and rarely left his home office.

As a way of socializing with other writers, editors, and agents, he had set up a regular Friday night nickel-dime poker game at his New York apartment. It wasn't the Deux-Magots in Paris or the Algonquin Round Table in New York, but for a wannabe author it was exhilarating to be among people devoted to writing.

Players would drop in any time, from after dinner until breakfast. We played games like High-Low Seven-Card Stud, Anaconda, and Iron Cross. And until I learned the subtleties of the games and the people at the table—when to bluff, when to fold—the tuition fee in this poker seminar left a gap in my fifty-dollar-a-week paycheck.

By 1953 the pulps suffered a serious decline in readership as a result of the new paperback books and television, and since Stadium Publications had to cut expenses, they gave me notice. Erisman would have to handle all the magazines by himself, using the house-name Arthur Lane to give the impression that a staff was still operating. The pulps soon vanished except for some of the science fiction magazines, like *Galaxy*, *Astounding*, and *The Magazine of Fantasy and Science Fiction*.

A few days before my job was terminated, Bob Erisman and I had lunch at Childs in the Empire State Building. We reminisced about working together. I leaned back after coffee and said, "Bob, I have a confession to make."

His eyebrows went up.

"Remember that writer whose stories you hated at first, and I told you I saw some talent in him?"

"You mean 'Bushwhack at Aransas Pass'?"

"Yeah. Well, I used a pen name and submitted that and all those other stories through an agent. I wanted you to know."

Bob smiled. "I guess confession is good for the soul. Remember those western and sports novels and novellas you weren't permitted to buy because they were written under contract?"

"Sure."

"Well, what do you think I was doing at home in Mystic, Connecticut, after I checked your work and wrote blurbs and titles?"

"You?"

He nodded.

We had a drink together and toasted the end of an era.

In contrast to the decline of the pulps, Martin Goodman Publications' subsidiary, *Timely Comics,* was flourishing. Goodman offered me a transfer, a job working for his son-in-law Stan Lee, who was in charge of the comic book line and has since become the head of a multimillion-dollar corporation called Marvel. Since my $17.25-a-month rent was almost due, I accepted what I considered a detour on my journey toward a literary career.

Stan Lee was a lanky, shy young man who kept pretty much to himself and let his editors deal with the scriptwriters, cartoonists, and lettering crew. Writers turned in plot synopses. Stan read them, and as a matter of course, would accept one or two from each of the regulars he referred to as his "stable." As one of his front men, I would pass along the comments and criticism. The writers would then develop them in script form, with dialogue and actions for each panel, much like movie screenplays.

Because of my experience editing *Marvel,* and because I'd sold a few science fiction stories by then, Stan allowed me to specialize in the horror, fantasy, suspense, and science fiction comic books. Naturally, I began submitting story ideas, getting freelance assignments, and supplementing my salary by writing the scripts on my own time.

One of the ideas I wrote, but didn't submit to him, I called "Brainstorm." It started out:

> The first guy in the test to raise the I.Q. from a low normal 90 to genius level . . . He goes through the experience, and then is thrown back to what he was . . . he is no brighter than he was before, but having had a sample of light, he can never be the same. The pathos of a man who knows what it is to be brilliant and to know that he can never again have the things that he tasted for the first time, including a brilliant, beautiful woman he fell in love with and with whom he can no longer have any contact.

I didn't submit it to Stan Lee because something told me it should be more than a comic book script. I knew I would do it someday after I learned how to write.

In the fall of 1952, in violation of Commandment Three—"Thou shalt not marry while in psychotherapy"—I proposed to Aurea and she accepted.

When I told Stan Lee about it, he rubbed his hands together and gloated. "That's great, Dan. Get married. Buy a house, take on a big mortgage. Buy a fancy car. Then you won't be so independent."

Phil and Morton Klass threw rice at Aurea and me as we left City Hall. A big wedding party at Peter Fland's Studio. Models and friends and a few relatives. The wedding cake was a cheesecake from Lindy's.

We didn't buy a house. We moved into my cold-water bachelor pad. Aurea was still working for Peter Fland, and I was once again trying to rewrite my Merchant Marine novel while free-lancing scripts for Stan.

A few months later, Aurea phoned, sounding upset. "Peter and his new partner are arguing. I think they're going to break up. You'd better come over and see that I get paid."

I left my writing desk, and went to the studio. Before the day was over, Aurea had left Fland. The partner had offered us a deal. He wanted Aurea as a photographer and fashion stylist and me as an advertising copywriter and salesman. We invested our savings in the fashion photography business and celebrated dreams of success.

Our partner, I soon discovered, seemed to be an incorrigible liar—at least that's what I believed at the time. I survived the year only by assuming that when he said it was nighttime, it was really daytime. The dream of business success turned into a recurrent nightmare. The partner is standing in front of me on a subway platform. I feel a rage. . . . I raise both hands and step forward. . . . Then another train, the elevated train of my childhood, thunders past my bed and I pull back, turn away, and hide under the covers. Never mind. I sold out to him, and we lost the savings we invested in the company.

No longer able to afford twice-weekly psychoanalysis sessions, I violated the Fourth Commandment by giving my therapist one fifty-minute-hour's notice.

I heard his voice from behind—actually speaking to me!

"You are a great mistake making. You, the rules knew when we started. You must pay for whatever appointments you for the rest of the month don't keep."

I got off the couch, looked him in the eye, and paid him. "Thanks for the memories."

Just as I later transformed my Tests and Measurements advisor into Burt the tester who administers the inkblot test to Charlie in "Flowers for Algernon," I see now that my ex-shrink was probably the model for Dr. Strauss.

For the purpose of exploring the writing life, let's set aside the current arguments for or against psychoanalysis. Over the years, as a writer, I have come to believe strongly in two of Freud's ideas: the power of the *unconscious* as a motivating force directing behavior, and his method of *free association* to plumb subconscious connections.

Since most writers use their own experiences to breathe life into their characters, and to create believable settings and actions, those two concepts provided me with ways to explore a lifetime accumulation of material, as well as the tools with which to retrieve them. My dream of becoming a writer grew out of my love of books and storytelling, but the only material I can really call my own is stored deep in the unconscious area of my root cellar. I use free association like a gardener's spade to dig out connected memories, bring them into the light, and replant them where they can bloom.

Many years later, when I was developing the novel version of *Flowers for Algernon,* I felt the book needed a psychoanalytic session between Dr. Strauss and Charlie. I struggled with it. Then, frustrated, I put it out of my mind. A few weeks later, I awoke early one morning, feeling the answer surfacing in my mind—coming close to the barrier. I lay there until the mental pictures came through—myself stretched out on my analyst's couch fighting to break through the Monday Morning Crust.

Although I didn't know it at the time, my shrink had earned his fee.

To write the scene, I just gave that memory to Charlie.

PART THREE

Mind over Matter

11

||||||||||||||||||||||

LOOKING FOR CHARLIE

DURING THE NEXT FEW MONTHS, the idea of artificially increasing human intelligence surfaced in my mind many times. It was a period of false starts, experiments, trial and error. Some of the early notes suggest opening episodes and different names for the main character.

||||||||||||||||||||

An officer recommends his cousin for the experiment of having his I.Q. changed. Walton is a bachelor who has long been in love with a girl who works in the tapes library . . .

||||||||||||||||||||

Steve Dekker has been in and out of prison more times than he can count. It seems that practically every time he pulls a job he gets caught. He has this self-defeating kind of personality that ends up in failure. He decides that this is because he's not smart enough—also there's a girl he's nuts about who won't give him a tumble, because he's not bright. So when he reads an article about making animals smarter he barges in and offers himself as a guinea-pig for brain surgery.

||||||||||||||||

The story of raising Flint Gargan's I.Q. Flint is a guy who is crude, enjoys scrawling dirty pix on bathroom walls, fights at the drop of a syllable . . . he's also filled with corny emotions, cries over sentimental gush, loves weddings, babies, dogs—has his own dog.

Flint hated school when he was a boy, left school to go out on his own as a plumber's helper . . . figures school's not so bad for some, but doesn't think that he would have been helped much by it.

||||||||||||||||

I try not to edit or judge while I'm writing. I let the raw material pour out, and if I feel it's good, I shape it later. But I didn't like Steve Dekker or Flint Gargan, and I wanted nothing more to do with them, or the dozens of other characters that appeared on my pages. I was searching my memory, my feelings, the world around me, for a clue to the character of this story.

I soon realized that part of my problem was that the story idea—the "What would happen if? . . ."—had come first, and now I was trying to cast an actor to play the role without knowing what he was like.

I decided to try working from the events that stemmed from the idea, and let the character evolve from the story.

The plot was developing through a sequence of connected episodes, the cause and effect chain of events, embodying what we call form or structure. But I was a long, long way from a story.

I tried starting later in the narrative, remembering Homer's epic strategy of starting "in the middle of the action," as in *The Iliad* and *The Odyssey*.

||||||||||||||||||

Three days later they wheeled him into the operating room of the Institute. He lifted himself up on one elbow and waved to Linda who had supervised his preparation.

"Wish me luck, beautiful," he said.

She laughed. "You'll be all right."

Dr. Brock's eyes smiled down at him from behind his surgical mask.

||||||||||||||||||

The fragment breaks off there, but if I were the editor, I'd have blue-penciled this with a note to the writer: "*'Smiling eyes?'* Watch your clichés. *'From behind his surgical mask'?*" If his eyes are smiling from behind the mask then he's going to operate blindfolded!

Still, part of that passage later found its way into the published novelette.

There are about twenty such attempts at beginnings, over several months. I had an idea I cared about. And a story line, and a few passages. But I still didn't have the character I felt was right. I was searching for a protagonist who would be memorable and with whom the reader and I could identify; someone with a strong motivation and goal who evoked a response from other characters; someone whose inner life gave him a human dimension.

Where would I find such a character? How could I invent and develop him? I hadn't the slightest idea.

Then, months later, he walked into my life and turned it around.

12

||||||||||||||||||||||

CHARLIE FINDS ME

IT HAPPENED IN BROOKLYN. Aurea and I moved back there, across the street from my parents' apartment, on the street where I'd grown up. We were broke. Aurea did freelance fashion styling and I resumed writing scripts for Stan Lee. Hundreds of them.

I took courses at night for a master's degree in American Literature to prepare myself for a teaching license as a way to buy my freedom from scriptwriting. I passed the Board of Education exam for substitute teacher, then taught at the high school from which I'd graduated ten years earlier.

I wrote nights, during the Christmas break, and summers. In 1956 I finished "The Trouble With Elmo," a science fiction story about a chess-playing super computer created to solve all the crises in the world. But the computer has figured out that when there are no more problems to solve, it will be destroyed. So Elmo solves every problem, but embeds what we would now call a computer "worm" or "Trojan horse" containing a program that creates new world crises for it to solve. "The Trouble With Elmo" appeared in *Galaxy* magazine.

———

I passed the New York Board of Education exam for an English teacher's license in June of 1957. With my higher salary as a regular teacher, Aurea and I were able to rent a one-bedroom house in Seagate, a gated community at the western tip of Coney Island. I loved strolling the beach, smelling the salt air, looking out at the ocean and recalling my seafaring days. I set up my typewriter and desk in a corner of the bedroom, confident I'd be able to write in this place.

The following school term, the chairman of the English department, impressed with my four published short stories, assigned me to teach two elective classes of creative writing. Each class was limited to twenty-five gifted students, all of whom loved reading and wanted to be writers. But many of them acted as if they deserved to have success handed to them because of their intelligence. When they groaned at the assignments and disdained revising their work, I told them, "There are those people *who want to write,* and others who *want to be writers.* For some geniuses, success comes without labor. For the rest of us, it's the love of writing that counts."

As if to compensate for these two "special classes," my other two classes were Special Modified English for low I.Q. students. For them, I was expected to concentrate on spelling, sentence structure, and developing paragraphs. Class discussions focused on issues of the day that might interest them. The key to teaching the "special" students in "modified classes," I was told, is to motivate them with things relevant to their own lives.

I will never forget my first day of teaching one of the Special Modified English classes. I can still see the boy, in the rear of the room near the window. When the school bell rings at the end of the 50-minute hour, students jump up and rush out—except that boy, who lumbers toward my desk. He wears a black parka, with the orange letter J.

"Mr. Keyes...Can I ask you something?"

"Sure. You on the football team?"

"Yeah. Linebacker. Look, Mr. Keyes, this is a dummy class, ain't it?"

I'm taken aback. "What?"

"A dummy class...for stupid people..."

Not knowing how to react, I mumble, "No...not really... It's just *special* and *modified.* We go a little slower than some of the other—"

"I know this is a dummy class, and I wanted to ask you. *If I try hard and I get smart by the end of the term, will you put me in a regular class? I want to be smart.*"

"Sure," I say, not knowing if I really have the authority. "Let's see what happens."

When I get home that evening, I try to work on a story I've started, but the boy keeps intruding. His words: *"I want to be smart"* haunt me to this day. It never occurred to me that a developmentally challenged person—in those days they called it *retarded*—would be aware of his or her limitations and might want to be more intelligent.

I began to write about him.

||||||||||||||

Short story of a boy in a modified class who begins to realize that he's a "dummy." Teacher's point of view. Donald...Title: "The Gifted and the Slow."

Two children who grow up near each other—one clever and the other dull. A slow child's deterioration a reflection of the entire culture. Stuart who is struggling against the knowledge that he is slow—Donald who abuses his intelligence.

||||||||||||||

A boy in a modified class—in love with a bright girl who—up to this point—doesn't understand the differences in intelligence. As each one becomes aware...He had been placed in this class after he became a behavior problem. He was in a gang of boys called the Cormorants.

||||||||||||||||

His teacher is a new, beginning teacher who has ideals and aspirations—and who believes that Corey can be straightened out. Corey is a neurotic boy—very bright but very disturbed. Bright boy comes into conflict with dull boy over a girl. The dull boy kills the bright boy in a fight.

||||||||||||||||

And so on...and so on...and so on...It was going nowhere. I put the notes away and forgot about them.

I decided to write a novel based on my experiences in the fashion photography business with Aurea and the partner who, I felt, nearly drove both of us crazy. She suggested that I take a leave of absence from teaching, and write full-time while she freelanced as a fashion stylist in Manhattan.

It went well. I was a night writer in those days, and the sound of my Royal typewriter in the bedroom lulled Aurea to sleep. In fact, if I stopped typing for too long she would awaken and mumble, "What's the matter?"

We'd have breakfast together, and then I would drive her to the train station on the back of my red Cushman scooter. I'd come back to the apartment for my day's sleep. Then I'd pick her up in the evening. We'd have dinner together. She would go to sleep, and I'd sit down at the typewriter in a corner of the bedroom.

I don't recall how long it took me to write the first draft of that fashion photography novel, but I do remember that after I put it away for a few days and then reread it, I was sick to my stomach. It was so bad.

I became depressed, frustrated, and demoralized—on the verge of giving up writing altogether.

Then, in the summer of 1958, H. L. Gold phoned and asked me to write a second story for *Galaxy* to follow "The Trouble With Elmo."

"I'll try, Horace. I've got an idea."

"Well, get it to me as soon as you can."

It's amazing how quickly depression, frustration, and demoralization can melt away when an editor asks a struggling writer for a story. I searched my files and notebooks.

There was that old, yellowed page from my first year at NYU with the line: *"I wonder what would happen if we could increase human intelligence artificially?"* I remembered my vision on the subway—*the wedge that intelligence has driven between me and my family.*

How often those thoughts have come back to me. I reread my notes and scraps about the operation to increase the I.Q., and the story idea, and the shape it might take—the plot of a classic tragedy.

Recalling Aristotle's dictum in his *Poetics,* that a tragedy can happen only to the highborn, because there can be a tragic fall only from a great height, I thought, let's test that. What if someone the world views as the lowest of the low, a mentally handicapped young man, climbs to the peak of Book Mountain, the heights of genius? And then loses it all. I felt myself choking up as I thought about it.

Okay, I've got the idea and the plot, I thought, but I still don't have the character with motivation.

I opened a more recent folder, turned several pages, and saw the note:

A boy comes up to me in the Special Modified English class and says, "I want to be smart."

Stunned, I stared at those pages, side by side. A motivation collided with a *"What would happen if...?"*

I glanced at Aurea, tossing restlessly in bed. I pushed my note folders aside ready to begin again. I needed new names. In the city she'd worked for the Larry *Gordon* Studio. Aurea's last boyfriend before we got married, my rival—his first name was *Charlie.*

I typed. Aurea sighed at the sound, and soon she was fast asleep.

Charlie Gordon—whoever you are, wherever you are—I hear you. I hear your voice calling out, *"Mr. Keyes, I want to be smart."*

Okay, Charlie Gordon, you want to be smart? I'll make you smart. Here I come, ready or not.

13

||||||||||||||||||||||

GETTING THERE

I TYPED THE FOLLOWING opening pages in one sitting, pounding away on the keys with more excitement writing than I'd ever known before. Here is the unedited first draft:

"The Genius Effect"
by Daniel Keyes

"What makes Gordon, here ideal for the experiment," said Dr. Strauss, "is that he has a low intelligence level and he's eager and willing to be made a guinea pig."

Charlie Gordon smiled and sat forward on the edge of his chair to hear what Dr. Nemur would answer to that.

"You may be right, Strauss, but he's such a small, frail looking thing. Can he take it, physically? We have no idea how much of a shock it will be to the human nervous system to have the intelligence level tripled in such a short time."

"I'm healthy," offered Charlie Gordon, rising and pounding on his slight chest. "I been working since I was a kid, and—"

"Yes, we know all about that, Charlie," said Dr. Strauss, motioning for Charlie to reseat himself. "What Doctor Nemur means is something else. It's too complicated to explain to you right now. Just relax, Charlie."

Turning his attention back to his colleague, Dr. Strauss continued: "I know he's not what you had in mind as the first of your new breed of intellectual supermen, but volunteers with seventy I.Q. are not easy to find. Most people of his low mentality are hostile and un-co-operative. An I.Q. of seventy usually means a dullness that's hard to reach.

"Charlie has a good nature and he's interested and eager to please. He knows that he's not bright, and he's begged me for the chance to serve as the subject of our experiment. You can't discount the value of motivation. You may be sure of yourself, Nemur, but you've got to remember that this will be the first human being ever to have his intelligence raised by surgical means."

Charlie didn't understand most of what Dr. Strauss was saying, but it sounded as if he were on his side. He held his breath as he waited for Dr. Nemur's answer. In awe, he watched the white-haired genius pull his upper lip over his lower one, scratch his ear and rub his nose. Then finally it came—a nod.

"All right," said Nemur, "we'll try him. Put him through the personality tests. I'll want a complete profile as soon as possible."

Unable to contain himself, Charlie Gordon leaped to his feet and reached across the desk to pump Dr. Nemur's hand. "Thank you, Doc, thank you. You won't be sorry for giving me a chance. I'll try hard to be smart. I'll try awful hard."

The first of the testers to encounter Charlie Gordon was a young Rorschach specialist who attempted to get a deeper insight into Charlie's personality.

"Now, Mr. Gordon," said the thin young man, pushing his glasses back on the bridge of his nose, "just tell me what you see on this card."

Charlie, who approached each new test with tension and the memory of many childhood failures, peered at the card suspiciously. "An inkblot."

"Yes, of course," smiled the tester.

Charlie got up to leave. "That's a nice hobby. I have a hobby too. I paint pictures, you know they have the numbers where you put the different colors—"

"Please, Mr. Gordon. Sit down. We're not through yet. Now what does it make you think of? What do you see in the inkblot?"

Charlie leaned closer to the card and stared at it intently. He took it from the tester's hand and held it close up. Then he held it far away from him glancing up at the young man out of the corner of his eye, hoping to get a hint. Suddenly, he was on his feet, heading out the door.

"Where are you going, Mr. Gordon?"

"To get my glasses."

When Charlie returned from the locker where he had left his glasses in his coat pocket, he explained. "I usually only have to use my glasses when I go to the movies or watch television, but they're really good ones. Let me see that card again. I'll bet I find it now."

Picking up the card again, he stared at it in disbelief. He was sure that he'd be able to see anything there with his glasses on. He strained and frowned and bit his nails. He wanted desperately to see what it was that the tester wanted him to find in that mass of inkblot. "It's an inkblot..." he said, but seeing the look of dismay on the young man's face, he quickly added, "but it's a nice one. Very pretty with these little things on the edges and..." He saw the young psychologist shaking his head and he let his voice trail off. Obviously he hadn't gotten it right.

"Mr. Gordon, now we know it's an inkblot. What I want you to tell me is what it makes you think of. What do you visualize—I mean what do you see in your mind when you look at it?"

"Let me try again," pleaded Charlie. "I'll get it in a few minutes. I'm not so fast sometimes. I'm a very slow reader too, but I'm trying hard." He took the card again and traced the outline of the blot for several minutes, his forehead knit in deep thought. "What does it remind me of? What does it remind me of...?" he mused to himself. Suddenly his forehead cleared. The young man leaned forward expectantly as Gordon said, "Sure—of course—what a dope I am. I should have thought of it before."

"Does it make you think of something?"

"Yes," said Charlie triumphantly, a knowing smile illuminating his face. "A fountain pen...leaking ink all over the tablecloth."

During the Thematic Apperception Test, in which he was asked to make up stories about the people and things he saw in a series of photographs, he ran into further difficulty.

"—I know you never met these people before," said the young woman who had done her Ph.D. work at Columbia, "I've never met them either. Just pretend that you—"

"Then if I never met them, how can I tell you stories about them? Now I've got some pictures of my mother and father and my little nephew Miltie. I could tell you stories about Miltie . . ."

He could tell by the way she was shaking her head sadly that she didn't want to hear stories about Miltie. He began to wonder what was wrong with all these people who asked him to do such strange things.

Charlie was miserable during the non-verbal intelligence tests. He was beaten ten times out of ten by a group of white mice who learned to work their way out of a maze before he did. It depressed him to learn that mice were so smart.

I remember typing that opening fragment. I saw myself writing my homework, the ink dripping from my pen, making an inkblot on the white paper, my mother's hand coming over my shoulder and ripping out the page. I laughed out loud as I saw it happening to Charlie, saw his reaction, heard his words. There was no thinking ahead. It was as if the sentences were flowing from my fingertips to the typewriter keys without passing through my brain. Something inside told me I had it. I finally had it.

Henry James wrote of the donnée—"the given"—as being the heart of the work given to the writer. Well, a boy had walked up to me and given me what I needed to spark the story, and, in return, I would give him some of my own memories to bring his character to life on the page.

Charlie's story had begun to tell itself. It felt right. It felt good.

Yet, the next evening, when I sat down to work, I couldn't go on. Something was blocking me. What? I knew the idea was original; I felt it was important; it had stayed with me over the years and demanded to be written. What was wrong?

As I reread the pages, I laughed aloud at Charlie's responses to the inkblot. Then, suddenly, it hit me. I was laughing *at* Charlie. The way I was telling the story, the reader would be laughing at Charlie. That's what most people did when they saw the mentally disadvantaged make mistakes. It was a way of making themselves feel superior. I remembered the day I broke the dishes, and the customers laughed and Mr. Goldstein called me *moron*.

I didn't want my readers to laugh at Charlie. Maybe laugh *with* him, but not *at* him.

Sure, I had the idea, and the plot, and the character, but I hadn't found the right way, the only way, to tell the story. The point of view, or what I prefer to call the *angle of vision*, was wrong. This had to be told from Charlie's perspective. It had to be first person, major character angle—in Charlie's mind and through Charlie's eyes all the way.

But how? What narrative strategy would let the story unfold?

Would the reader believe that a developmentally disadvantaged person could write this as a memoir from beginning to end? I couldn't believe that myself. I liked the idea of each event, each scene, being recorded as it was happening, or right after it had happened. Diary? Again, not plausible that—at least in the beginning and at the end—Charlie would sit down and make long journal entries.

I struggled with the narrative strategy for several days, growing more and more frustrated, because I felt I was so close to unlocking the story. Then one morning I awoke with the answer in my mind. As part of the experiment, Charlie would be asked to keep an ongoing record, a *progress report*.

I had never heard the term before, or read a story or novel in which it had been used. I suspected that I was developing a unique point of view.

Now that I had found Charlie's voice, I knew he would tell it through my fingers on the keys. But how would I handle the sentence structure and spelling? Students in my modified classes provided the model. How would I know how he thought? I would try to remember what it was like to be a child. How would I know his feelings? I would give him my feelings.

When Flaubert was asked how he could have imagined and written of life through the mind of a woman in *Madame Bovary,* his answer was: *"I am Madame Bovary."*

In that sense, I gave Charlie Gordon some of myself, and I became part of that character.

Still, I was worried about opening with the illiterate spelling and short, childish sentence structure. I wondered about the reader's reaction. Then I remembered what Mark Twain did in *The Adventures of Huckleberry Finn.* Before plunging into the vernacular of the uneducated Huck, Twain alerts the reader with the author's educated voice.

The novel opens with a "NOTICE": "Persons attempting to find a motive in this narrative will be prosecuted; persons attempting to find a moral in it will be banished; persons attempting to find a plot in it will be shot.

"BY ORDER OF THE AUTHOR, Per G. G., Chief of Ordnance."

This is followed by an EXPLANATORY:

"In this book a number of dialects are used, to wit: the Missouri Negro dialect, the extremest form of the backwoods Southwestern dialect, the ordinary 'Pike County' dialect, and four modified varieties of this last..." signed "THE AUTHOR."

Only then, after having prepared the reader, does Twain begin the first-person narrative from Huck's point of view and in his voice.

You don't know about me without you have read a book by the name of *The Adventures of Tom Sawyer,* but that ain't no matter. That book was made by Mr. Mark Twain and he told the truth, mainly. There was things which he stretched, but mainly he told the truth.

I decided to follow Twain's strategy. My original opening— which I later deleted and can no longer find—begins with Alice Kinnian coming to the lab and asking Professor Nemur if he has heard from Charlie. Nemur hands her the manuscript, the first pages of which are written in pencil, pressed so hard she can feel the words raised on the back of the paper.

Only then does Charlie's voice take over as I type:

<blockquote>

progris riport 1—martch 5

Dr. Strauss says I shud rite down what I think and evrey thing that happins to me from now on. I dont know why but he says its importint so they will see if they will use me. I hope they use me. Miss Kinnian says maybe they can make me smart. I want to be smart. My name is Charlie Gordon. I am 37 years old and 2 weeks ago was my brithday. I have nuthing more to rite now so I will close for today.

</blockquote>

When I saw those words on the page, I knew I had it. I wrote through that night and the nights that followed, feverishly, long hours, little sleep and lots of coffee.

Then, in the middle of the night, partway through the first draft, after the scene in which Charlie races the white mouse, I called out loud, *"The mouse! The mouse!"*

Aurea jumped up, startled. "Where? Where?"

I explained and she smiled sleepily, "Oh, good."

I turned back to the typewriter and typed a note to myself:

The mouse, having had the same treatment as Charlie, will forecast events connected with the experiment. It will be a character in its own right, and a furry little sidekick for Charlie.

A name—I had to give the mouse a name. My fingers went over the keys. It just appeared on the page. Algernon.

After that, the story wrote itself, about thirty thousand words—what would be called a long novelette or a short novella.

In that first complete draft, the story ends with Alice Kinnian looking up from the folder of progress reports with tears in her eyes, and asking Professor Nemur to go with her to help find Charlie.

Phil Klass (William Tenn) by this time had moved with his wife, Fruma, into an apartment across the street from me in Seagate. Phil was the next person to read the story after Aurea. When he returned the manuscript the next day, he said, "This will be a classic."

I knew he was teasing me, and I laughed.

My next move was to get a different literary agent. I phoned Harry Altshuler, introduced myself, and told him of H. L. Gold's request that I write a second story for *Galaxy*. Altshuler asked to read "Flowers for Algernon," and I sent it to him. He said he liked it, and would be pleased to be my agent. H. L. Gold should, of course, have first crack at it.

Euphoria is a mild word to describe my feelings. I had just finished a story that had been in the back of my mind for years, and I felt good about it. And I had landed a respected agent who liked it and an editor who had asked for it. My troubles, I thought, were over.

I was mistaken.

14

||||||||||||||||||||||

REJECTION AND ACCEPTANCE

A FEW DAYS LATER, Harry Altshuler called and told me he'd been in touch with H. L. Gold on behalf of another of his writers, and had mentioned my new story. "Horace wants you to bring it to his office-apartment. He'll read it right away. Do you know his place?"

"It's where I learned to play poker and discovered I'm not very good at bluffing."

"All right then. Don't discuss price if he wants to buy it. I'll handle that end."

It was a long trip from Coney Island to Fourteenth Street on the east side of Manhattan, and by the time I arrived I was on edge. The story meant a lot to me, and I hoped it could be published in a major science fiction magazine like *Galaxy*. But Horace had a reputation as a hands-on editor who didn't hesitate to ask for changes.

He greeted me at the door, took the envelope, and said, "Relax in the study while I read this in my office. Help yourself to coffee and doughnuts."

It had never occurred to me that he would read it while I

waited, or that I would get instant feedback from one of the most prestigious editors in the field.

For the next hour or so, I drank coffee, read the *New York Times,* and stared into space wondering if he would like it or hate it, buy it or reject it. Finally, he came out of his office, deep in thought, and sat across from me.

"Dan, this is a good story. But I'm going to suggest a few changes that will turn it into a great story."

I don't remember how I responded.

"The ending is too depressing for our readers," he said. "I want you to change it. Charlie doesn't regress. He doesn't lose his intelligence. Instead, he remains a super-genius, marries Alice Kinnian, and they live happily ever after. That would make it a great story."

I stared at him. How does a beginning writer respond to the editor who bought one story from him, and wants to buy a second? The years of labor over this story passed through my mind. What about my Wedge of Loneliness? My tragic vision of Book Mountain? My challenge to Aristotle's theory of the Classic Fall?

"I'll have to think about it," I mumbled. "I'll need a little time."

"I'd like to buy it for one of the upcoming issues, but I'd need that revision. It shouldn't take you long."

"I'll work on it," I said, knowing there was no way I'd change the ending.

"Good," he said, showing me to the door. "If not, I'm sure you'll write other stories for *Galaxy* in the future."

I called Harry Altshuler from a pay phone and told him what had happened. There was a long pause.

"You know," he said, "Horace is a fine editor, with a strong sense of the market. I agree with him. It shouldn't be too hard to make that change."

I wanted to shout: *This story has a piece of my heart in it!* But who was I to pit my judgment against professionals? The train ride back to Seagate was long and depressing.

When I told Phil Klass what had happened, he shook his head. "Horace and Harry are wrong. If you dare to change the ending, I'll get a baseball bat and break both your legs."

"Thanks."

He made another suggestion. He was then working for Bob Mills, editor of *The Magazine of Fantasy and Science Fiction*. "Let me take the story up to Mills and see if he'll buy it."

I was torn. Whereas *Galaxy* was considered the most successful science fiction magazine, *F&SF* was most respected for its literary merit. I told Phil to go ahead.

A few days later I got the good news along with the bad. Bob Mills liked the story and wanted to publish it, but he was limited by the publisher to a maximum of 15,000 words per story. If I'd agree to cut 10,000 words, he would buy it at two cents a word.

"I'll see," I said.

The decision wasn't too hard. Recalling my own editing days, Bob Erisman's admonition to cut, and Meredith's comment that Lester del Rey would never revise because it would cut his income in half, I shook each page, and crossed out every paragraph and word that wasn't absolutely necessary. It didn't hurt as much as I feared.

I got rid of *that-ery* and *which-ery,* and redundant phrases, and digressions. *"Sentences plodding along with lots of little words just like this one does were revised."* Changed to read: *"I revised plodding sentences."* Fifteen words trimmed to four without changing the meaning. At the same time, by altering *were revised* to *I revised*—passive voice to active voice—I changed pedestrian style into a lean, muscular prose.

Then I looked at the last scene in which Alice puts down the manuscript and asks Nemur to go with her to find Charlie. I hesitated a moment, and then drew a long diagonal line through that page and a half, allowing the story to end with his words: *"P. P. S. Please if you get a chanse put some flowrs on Algernons grave in the bak yard..."*

Bob Mills bought the story.

That summer, I was invited to attend one of the getaway workshops in Milford, Pennsylvania, at which the old-guard Hydra Club writers were invited to spend part of each afternoon passing around pages of new stories for critique by their professional peers. I was invited to submit a story for the workshop, and I decided to let them read "Flowers for Algernon."

The night before the workshop, I glanced through the manuscript and realized I'd made a mistake. Since I'd cut off the ending, in which Alice finishes reading the progress reports and goes off in search of Charlie, the opening, in which Nemur gives her the manuscript, was now superfluous.

I'd written it that way because I was afraid to let the story open with Charlie's illiterate spelling and simple plodding sentences. I'd been afraid to throw the reader into Charlie's "special" point of view without warning.

I decided I had to trust the reader.

That night, I cut the first two pages and let the story begin with Charlie's words, in Charlie's voice:

progris riport 1—martch 5

Dr. Strauss says I shud rite down what I think and evrey thing that happins to me from now on. I dont know why but he says its importint so they will see if they will use me. I hope they use me.

Then I went out to face my critics. Among those I remember forty years later, were Judy Merrill, Damon Knight, Kate Wilhelm, Jim Blish, Avram Davidson, Ted Cogswell, Gordie Dickson. I beg those I haven't mentioned to forgive me.

We set out chairs on the front lawn, and then passed the pages around the circle. All I can remember now is the generous warm praise, the congratulations, and the sense that these people I admired had accepted me as a fellow writer.

"Flowers for Algernon" was published as the lead story of the April 1959 issue of *The Magazine of Fantasy and Science Fiction*, with a cover by Ed Emshwiller. Five months later, he gave Aurea the original oil painting as a gift in honor of the birth of our first child, Hillary Ann. The painting still hangs in our living room.

At the Eighteenth World Science Fiction Convention in Pittsburgh, in 1960, as Isaac Asimov handed me the Hugo Award for the Best Story of 1959, he praised it lavishly.

Asimov later wrote in *The Hugo Winners:*

'How did he do it?' I demanded of the Muses. 'How did he do it?'... And from the round and gentle face of Daniel Keyes, issued the immortal words: 'Listen, when you find out how I did it, let me know, will you. I want to do it again.'

I wasn't alone on that celebration night. An unseen someone cast a second shadow in the spotlight beside me. Another hand reached out for the Hugo Award. Out of the corner of my mind, I glimpsed a memory of the boy who had walked up to my desk and said, "Mr. Keyes, I want to be smart."

And he has been with me as Charlie Gordon ever since.

PART FOUR

||||||||||||||||||||||

The Alchemy of Writing

15

||||||||||||||||||||

TRANSFORMATIONS: FROM STORY TO TELEPLAY TO NOVEL

SHORTLY AFTER "FLOWERS FOR ALGERNON" won the Hugo Award, CBS bought TV rights for the Theater Guild's *U.S. Steel Hour* teleplay. James Yaffee, author of the novel *Compulsion*, wrote the script. Cliff Robertson played the role of Charlie.

Three weeks after I received my M.A. degree in English and American Literature from Brooklyn College, on the evening of Washington's birthday, I saw *The Two Worlds of Charlie Gordon* from beside Aurea's bed in the hospital where she was recovering from an illness.

Nurses gathered to watch, crowding the room and blocking the doorway. They applauded when my name appeared in the screen credits, and again when the show ended. I pulled out a bottle of champagne I had smuggled in, and filled the little plastic medicine cups the head nurse provided. There were toasts and sips all around.

Cliff Robertson's performance was stunning, so I wasn't surprised at the rave reviews the next day, or the nomination for the Emmy Award. Later, when *The Two Worlds of Charlie Gordon* lost, it was to *Macbeth*, starring Maurice Evans.

A few days after the telecast, Cliff Robertson began negotiations for theatrical movie rights. As he told the press, he'd been "...always a bridesmaid but never a bride," referring to his TV performances in *Days of Wine and Roses* and *The Hustler.* He had lost those starring movie roles, he said, to Jack Lemmon and Paul Newman.

Six months later, Robertson and I closed the deal. He was going to follow his TV success with a movie retitled, *Charly,* its childlike printing with a backward *R.*

Lest the reader have the mistaken notion that all of this is the financial equivalent of winning the lottery, let me put things into perspective by revealing to you my 1961 writing income, after the 10 percent agents' deductions, all from "Flowers for Algernon":

2/10—*Best Articles and Stories* reprint	$4.50
4/24—*The Best from Fantasy and Science Fiction*	$22.50
9/8—Movie option from Robertson Associates	$900.00
11/2—*Literary Cavalcade* reprint	$22.50
Total Net:	$949.50

So I had to continue teaching high school days to support my wife and child while I wrote nights.

One afternoon, while I was on the train headed home from Thomas Jefferson High School, a colleague sat down beside me.

"Dan, I read 'Flowers for Algernon,' a fine novelette," he said. "I've been wondering about some of the images and their meanings."

Recognition is sweet.

He mentioned something he'd noticed, was sure it had a symbolic meaning, and asked me to elaborate.

I did. I pontificated on the levels of meanings, the central and peripheral symbolic motifs.

When I was done, he looked at me quizzically, eyebrows raised. *"Oh...,"* he said, *"is that all?"*

His words are branded somewhere in my writer's psyche. Since then, I have never explained, explicated, or interpreted my work, its meanings, its levels, its themes. My colleague had taught me a lesson. As long as the writer, or any artist for that matter, keeps his mouth shut, there can be argument and discussion and various interpretations and meanings. But once the writer explains or analyzes, he trivializes his own work.

Although in this book I am describing writing methods, sources, and the creative process, I no longer explain. That's the reader's contribution.

Well, now that some critics have proclaimed that writers don't really know what they're doing, much less understand their own works, it's best we keep silent about our intentions.

What do I mean? Never mind.

While all this was going on, I began a second version of a novel I'd 'worked on based on my Merchant Marine experiences. Someone once said, "The way you learn to write a novel is by writing a novel." And, I thought, the way to learn to write a novel better is to do it over.

During a break in the writing, I read an article in *Life* magazine about an accident in an industrial plant that used radioactive isotopes. There were photographs of the technician who had been contaminated, and of his home where decontamination specialists had cut away parts of the rug and drapes because he'd unknowingly tracked particles of radioactive dust into his home.

I was saddened by the pictures of his wife, whose hair had to be cropped, and of the son, who had developed radiation sickness. Their expressions moved me.

In the winter of 1961, I put aside the Merchant Marine novel and began *A Trace of Dust*, a novel about the effects of an industrial radiation spill on Barney and Karen Stark, a young couple who—after many disappointments—are finally expecting their first child. How would the community react to having been contaminated? How would Karen endure her pregnancy, wondering if she would give birth to a mutant? This was long before it was possible to examine a fetus in the uterus.

Usually, as I work on a story, it crowds in on me during nonwriting hours, and I compose and edit and revise. But once it's published, I go on to other things—if I'm lucky, to other writing. But I discovered that something else was going on in my mind at the same time—Charlie Gordon was haunting me.

Although I had set aside the sea novel to sketch out the radiation novel, changing the title to *The Contaminated Man*, Charlie kept surfacing. I was recalling scenes from his childhood, memories of his parents, of his normal sister, other events during his growing up. I jotted down notes, and put them aside. I stayed with the radiation novel, now calling it *The Midas Touch*. I had already become wise to the tricks the writer's mind plays on itself. There you are, writing along, smooth sailing, and then you get another idea you're sure is better than the one you're working on. It feels so hot it demands to be written, but after you start that one, you get another idea, and then another, and before you know it you've got a chain of unfinished works. How do I know this? I've got dozens of them. Are they dead or just dormant in my root cellar? I won't know until I try to replant them.

I tried resisting Charlie Gordon, but he wouldn't let up. He *demanded* my attention. I remember sitting at my typewriter one summer's day, when I had an unexpected thought.

As a super-genius, Charlie would probably have total recall of scenes and events back to his childhood. But, I wondered, how would he have perceived his childhood world before the experiment? Blurred? Incomplete? And then, after his transformation, how would genius Charlie recall those gauzy visions?

That would be a writing challenge.

I wanted to write it, but I didn't want to set aside the radioactive contamination novel, now called *The Touch*.

I was already wondering with apprehension whether or not the child of Barney and Karen Stark would be born a mutant.

Finally, in desperation, I wrote an opening chapter of *The Touch*, and also a plan for work to develop the novelette "Flowers for Algernon" into a full-length novel.

Which should I do first?

I told myself, developing *Flowers for Algernon* shouldn't take too long. I had the idea, plot, main characters, point of view, and the narrative strategy of Charlie's progress reports. Since it was merely a matter of letting it grow, of filling in more details, I probably should do it first. Considering it had won the Hugo Award, I should be able to get an advance from a book publisher.

I put aside *The Touch*. On the basis of my plan to develop *Flowers for Algernon*, a publisher offered me a book contract with an advance of $650. If the manuscript was unacceptable, or if I didn't meet the deadline, I would have to return the full amount. I had never before written with a deadline, and I knew I would need free time to work on it.

I'd heard of published authors teaching creative writing at colleges and universities with only an M.A. degree. If I could find a position somewhere in higher education, it would mean giving up my regular New York teaching license and tenure, in exchange for a six- to nine-hour a week schedule.

I sent out a hundred inquiries to colleges across the country, seeking a teaching position, and I received one positive response. Wayne State University in Detroit offered me a four-year lectureship—nonrenewable, nontenurable—to teach literature and creative writing. I would have two classes a quarter, each meeting twice weekly for three hours, plus conferences.

As I struggled with the decision, I recalled Shakespeare's words:

> *There is a tide in the affairs of men,*
> *Which taken at the flood, leads on to fortune;*
> *Omitted, all the voyage of their life*
> *Is bound in shallows and in miseries.*
> *On such a full sea are we now afloat;*
> *And we must take the current when it serves,*
> *Or lose our ventures.*
> *Julius Caesar,* act 4, scene 3

Shakespeare was right. The time was now. I had to take the risk. I assured myself, it shouldn't take long to flesh out the novelette to a full-length novel. Then I could return to *The Touch.*

I purchased an ancient car from a teaching colleague, and loaded it with most of our possessions. With my wife's encouragement, a grubstake from the movie option, and the publisher's advance, we set out—Aurea, three-year-old Hillary, and I.

As we drove through the Lincoln Tunnel, I thought of Mr. Ochs of the *New York Times,* and his advice to his son and me. "Westward Ho, Charlie!" I called out. "It's *Flowers for Algernon* or bust!"

16

||||||||||||||||||||

Rejected Again

For the next two years, while I taught at Wayne State, *Flowers for Algernon* was growing into a full-length novel. There was so much in Charlie's life I wanted to explore. Yet, I was apprehensive. The response to the novelette had been so strong that I feared people would resent my tampering with it. But I had no choice. Charlie was driving me.

Characters I'd merely named or briefly sketched in the novelette, because there hadn't been space or time to show them in action, I now developed in scenes.

I was no longer satisfied with the setting of Charlie's job. I felt the paper box factory, where I had worked as a boy, was too dull. The novel needed a place where the sights and smells would be more vivid. It would have to be a place I knew well.

Going through old notes and papers, I found the descriptive sketch of the bakery I'd written long ago, and I changed Charlie's job.

In the novel version, I used some—not all—of the bakery images from that sketch, but not the process of baking bagels. At that time, the early 1960s, bagels were not as ubiquitous as they are now. Anyway, a writer never uses it all. Just what's needed to tell the story.

In addition to remembered images, characters like the real Gimpy, with his clubfoot, and the flour in the seams of his shoes and on his hands and in his hair, came to life.

But something happens when a writer gives real memories to characters to make them come alive. Since emotions facilitate the transfer of scenes and images—along with their feelings—to long-term memory, I've discovered that when I transfer those moments to my fictional characters, I often lose the emotions connected with them. Like the heart-shaped locket and the real event behind it. Anyone who has read only the novelette may ask, "What heart shaped locket?" It's in the novel, but not in the novelette.

In the short version, I was primarily concerned with Charlie's intellectual growth. Now, probing deeper into his mind and his past, I needed to understand experiences that had shaped his emotional growth.

In the novel, Charlie remembers what happened at P. S. 13, and why they had to transfer him to another school. He had found a gold locket in the street. No chain, so he's tied a string to it, and he likes to see the locket twirl. On Valentine's Day, the other boys tell about the cards they're going to buy for a popular girl named Harriet. Since Charlie has no money, he decides to give her the heart-shaped locket.

He takes tissue paper and ribbon from his mother's dresser drawer, and asks his friend Hymie to print on a card: *"Dear Harriet, I think your the most prettiest girl in the whole world. I like you very much and I love you. I want you to be my valentine. Your friend, Charlie Gordon."*

But, unknown to Charlie, his friend Hymie writes something else—a "dirty note"—and says, "Boy, this will knock her eyes out. Wait'll she sees this."

Charlie follows Harriet home from school, and when she goes inside he hangs the locket and note on the outside doorknob, rings the bell, and runs away. He's happy because he thinks she will wear it to school next day and tell all the boys he gave it to her.

But she doesn't wear the locket, and the next day her two older brothers confront Charlie in the school yard.

"You keep away from my kid sister, you degenerate. You don't belong in this school anyway."

Oscar pushes Charlie over to Gus, who catches him by the throat. Charlie is scared and starts to cry. Oscar punches him in the nose, and Gus knocks him on the ground and kicks him and then both of them kick him. His clothes are torn and his nose is bleeding and one of his teeth is broken, and after Gus and Oscar go away he sits on the sidewalk and cries. He tastes blood....

That scene and the emotion behind it comes from my own boyhood. Once, as I walked home after visiting my aunt, I was surrounded by a gang of boys much older, much bigger than me. What was I doing in their neighborhood? they wanted to know. But before I could answer, I was beaten, tossed from one to another, punched and kicked and bloodied. Over the years, that memory surfaced often with emotions of fear and hatred.

I combined that memory with another one, and gave it to Charlie.

Earlier—I must have been eight or nine—there was a girl all the boys had a crush on. She was pretty and coy and she teased us.

I had a small heart-shaped locket I'd found, and I left it on her doorknob on Valentine's Day. I didn't get beaten up by her brothers—she had no brothers—but my mother and I were called to the principal's office the next day, and he reprimanded me.

I blended the beating and the locket memories, added my re-called image of a boy who used to stand in front of his parents' store playing with a string threaded with buttons and beads, twirling them, back and forth, back and forth.

These elements, and probably a few others, like my transfer to another school, I gave to Charlie to make him come alive.

Then something strange happened.

As I wrote that scene, the emotions connected to the memories began to drain away. I no longer felt the fear, the pain, the embarrassment I had experienced at the time. Ever since the writing, those memories and emotions have belonged to Charlie. They're no longer mine.

F. Scott Fitzgerald alludes to something like this in a self-revealing article called, I think, "Handle with Care." He describes the writer holding an empty rifle, suggesting that—in having given away parts of himself—he is finally empty. He speaks of having overdrawn his emotional bank account. The cost of creating living characters out of himself has drained him.

Because of my own experiences, I have often been troubled with that thought. But I reassure myself that as long as a writer is working, and open to new emotional experiences, he is restocking his memory's bank account.

For example, my visit to the place I fictionalized as the "Warren State Home and Training School."

At one point during the revision, I realized the novel needed something I hadn't dealt with in the story version: The genius Charlie would surely be concerned with his future as well as his past.

Near the end of Progress Report 15, he says to Nemur, *"I might as well know everything while I'm still in a position to have some say about it. What plans have you made for me?"*

Nemur shrugs. *"The Foundation has arranged to send you to the Warren State Home and Training School."*

Charlie is upset at the thought and decides to visit the place. When Nemur asks why, Charlie says, *"Because I want to see. I've*

*got to know what's going to happen while I'm still enough in control
to be able to do something about it..."*

I hadn't imagined that idea before Charlie said those words on
paper. It wasn't part of the original plan for work. But now that
my character wanted to know what was to become of him, I had
to know too.

Since I'd never seen a state facility for what is now referred to as
the *developmentally challenged* and knew nothing about them, I
wrote letters to several institutions giving my background, explaining my purpose, and asking for permission to visit.

I was invited. I spent the day. Then I wrote the scene.

JULY 14—It was a bad day to go out to Warren—gray and
drizzly—and that may account for the depression that
grips me when I think about it.

From that opening line, the seven-page episode in Progress
Report 16, during which Charlie tours Warren, is a record of my
own emotions during that visit.

The people Charlie meets, the sights Charlie sees, are what I
discovered that day. He meets Winslow, the young head psychologist, with the tired look on his face, but the suggestion of
strength behind the youthful expression; the sympathetic nurse
with the wine-colored birthmark on the left side of her face; the
stuttering teacher of the woodworking class of deaf mutes he
called his "silent boys"; the motherly principal.

But I was most moved when I saw one of the bigger boys
cradling an older, more severely handicapped boy in his arms.

Thinking through Charlie's mind as he tries to imagine what
it will be like walking through these corridors as a patient, I gave
him my emotional responses.

Progress Report 16: I visualized myself in the middle of a line of men and boys waiting to enter a classroom. Perhaps I'd be one of those pushing another boy in a wheelchair, or guiding someone else by the hand, or cuddling a smaller boy in my arms.

Winslow, the head psychologist, says he didn't hire a psychiatrist because: *"... at the price I'd have to pay I'm able to hire two psychologists—men who aren't afraid to give away a part of themselves to these people."*

"What do you mean by 'a part of themselves'?"

He studied me for a moment, and then through the tiredness flashed an anger. "There are a lot of people who will give money or materials, but very few who will give time and affection. That's what I mean." His voice grew harsh, and he pointed to an empty baby bottle on the bookshelf across the room. ... "How many people do you know who are prepared to take a grown man into his arms and let him nurse with the bottle? And take the chance of having the patient urinate or defecate all over him?"

As I drove out of Warren, I didn't know what to think. The feeling of cold grayness was everywhere around me ... I may soon be coming to Warren to spend the rest of my life with the others ... waiting.

This is what I mean by restocking a writer's memory banks. I visited the place, met the people, experienced the emotions, and then gave them away. Now, it's Charlie's voice, Charlie's thoughts, Charlie's feelings. Although I had them first, they're no longer mine.

Development of the novel didn't go as quickly as I had expected. It took a year before I was ready to send it to the publisher. Yet, I made my deadline, and I felt good about my work.

The editor didn't.

I'll omit his name, and say only that he's no longer an editor. He's become a well-known literary agent.

He returned the manuscript, saying, *it wasn't acceptable in its present form.* He felt the book suffered from expansion. He said it was a remarkable short story, and a great deal of the quality remained. But no new elements had been added, he wrote, to give it a new dimension.

He had other criticisms: He found the sections about Charlie's sister, and some of the other dreams, "disturbing and much too strong stuff for this category." He complained about the lack of confrontation between Charlie and the professors. He insisted that the reader would expect a real duel between them and would be disappointed without one. Besides that, he said, it really needed more drama in the present—a new plotline. He suggested that Charlie and Burt the tester might both be in love with Alice Kinnian.

All he was asking me to do was to rewrite it completely, changing it into a formula love triangle superimposed on the plot of a hero/villain "duel."

And, most cutting of all (*pun intended*), he thought the manuscript needed to be cut substantially. *Déjà vu.*

Luckily, my experience with H. L. Gold's suggestions for making it a *great story* by having Charlie keep his intelligence, marry Alice, and live happily ever after, had strengthened my resolve to protect what I had created.

There's no point in trying to describe my despair. I taught my creative writing courses in a daze for the next week. I wanted my novel published, but I had no intention of making those changes. I picked my emotions up off the floor, wiped the blood off my psyche, and went back to work.

I would revise, but only what I felt Charlie and the story itself demanded.

17

||||||||||||||||||||||||

OF LOVE AND ENDINGS

UP TO THAT POINT in the writing, the form of the story had
been a single curve, tracing Charlie's intelligence rising to a peak,
and then falling as he deteriorates.

Perhaps the novel did need a second curve, an emotional
curve. And, of course, it would lag behind his intelligence curve,
creating a different kind of conflict between himself and Alice.
But not a love triangle!

It had to start with adolescent romantic yearnings, and I
didn't have to dig too deep into myself to give Charlie those shy
and awkward moments in my youth. Since their roots were in
my memories, I felt they would find resonance with most young
people awakening to love.

When Charlie takes Alice to a concert, he is unsure of himself:

*I had no way of knowing what she expected of me. This was
far from the clear lines of problem-solving and the systematic
acquisition of knowledge. I kept telling myself that the sweating palms, the tightness in my chest, the desire to put my arms
around her were merely bio-chemical reactions... Should I or*

*not? Was she waiting for me to do it? Would she get angry? I
could tell I was still behaving like an adolescent and it an-
gered me.*

Following Alice's rejection of Charlie's fumbling attempts to
show affection, I created a new scene to reveal their emotional
interaction:

[She says,] *"But you're changing emotionally too. In a pecu-
liar sense I'm the first woman you've ever been really aware
of—in this way. Up to now I've been your teacher—someone
you turn to for help and advice. You're bound to think you're
in love with me. See other women. Give yourself more time."*

*"What you're saying is that young boys are always falling in
love with their teachers, and that emotionally I'm still just
a boy."*

*"You're twisting my words around. No, I don't think of you
as a boy."*

"Emotionally retarded then."

"No."

"Then why?"

*"Charlie, don't push me. I don't know. Already, you've gone
beyond my intellectual reach. In a few months or even weeks,
you'll be a different person. When you mature intellectually, we
may not be able to communicate. When you mature emotionally, you may not even want me. I've got to think of myself too,
Charlie. Let's wait and see. Be patient."*

I see now that by throwing myself back into the work, I was
transforming my despair at being rejected by my editor into
Charlie's emotional upheaval as Alice rejects his fumbling, adolescent displays of affection.

It left me feeling much better about the novel. Instead of pre-fabricating a formula love triangle, I was letting it grow out of the story.

I drew on my courtship and marriage to Aurea for the emotions. As I was laboring over this new dimension of the novel, in February of 1964, Aurea was giving birth to our second daughter, Leslie Joan.

Meanwhile, Cliff Robertson, who was trying to get the movie version under way, insisted on seeing the novel manuscript. I told him it wasn't ready yet. From time to time, as he flew from his New York home to Hollywood, he would phone me to meet him at the Detroit Airport. We would have lunch or dinner.

During one of these meetings, we talked about his performance in the television version, *The Two Worlds of Charlie Gordon*. I told him about H. L. Gold's attempt to get me to change the ending for *Galaxy,* and how glad I was that I had resisted. "But I've seen many *U.S. Steel Hour* shows," I said, "and I don't ever recall seeing a downbeat ending before this. How was it possible to keep the teleplay ending so close to the novelette?"

Here's what he told me:

He and the scriptwriter had wanted to stay true to the story, but the producers at the Theater Guild as well as its *U.S. Steel Hour* sponsors had said that the downbeat ending didn't fit the mold of their hour-long teleplays.

After much wrangling, Robertson said, they came up with a compromise. As he knelt beside Algernon's grave in the backyard, he was to pick up the book with the blue cover—I recall it was Milton's *Paradise Lost*—which he was no longer able to read. He was to turn a few pages, register surprise, then excitement, lips moving as he silently started to read it. An upturn, to suggest that his intelligence was returning.

"Cliff, I saw the show," I said. "I didn't see that."

"*The U.S. Steel Hour* was *live television,* Dan. Charlie just wouldn't let me do it."

He knew he'd been instructed to do the upturn, to hint at a happy ending, he said. But he was so deep into the character that he just sat there, frozen until the OFF THE AIR sign lit up. "They were all furious!" he said. "You can't imagine the names they called me. They shouted, 'You're through!' 'You'll never act on TV again!'"

But the rave reviews the next day, and the Emmy Award nomination changed all that, he said, and led to his buying the movie rights for himself. Now, he'd hired a young writer to do a screenplay. Would I care to read it?

"Sure," I said, pleased at his story of the TV ending.

Then he leaned back thoughtfully. "Of course, Dan, you realize that in a full-length feature movie, we can't have a downbeat ending. The audience could never handle that."

Uh-oh...I thought, here we go again.

Robertson leaned over the table. "How would it be if Algernon doesn't die? At the end of the movie, when he's lying in a corner of the maze, we *think* he's dead..."

I sat there frozen.

"Then, as the camera pans in," he said, "and focuses on Algernon, he lifts his snout, wiggles his whiskers, and takes off running the maze. Just a *little* upbeat ending—"

"Cliff, I'd rather not hear any more," I said, tossing down my napkin. "I'm still working on the novel. It's your movie. I've got no control over what you do with the ending, but leave me out of it."

Four months later, on June 5, 1964, the editor wrote that he didn't care to publish the second version because I hadn't solved the problems he'd raised. He suggested that I try to sell the book to a paperback house, and if I made the sale, I would have to return the advance. He added, "If that doesn't work out, we can discuss a relatively painless way for Mr. Keyes to return the $650."

After the shock wore off, I thought, well, that's that!—as far as this editor and publisher were concerned. I was opposed to the idea of selling it as a paperback original. I had put too much of myself into it to go that route. I wanted my first novel to have the respect and attention reviewers accord a hardcover trade edition.

Although I was still willing to discuss ideas or possible changes with an editor who liked it for what it was, I decided I had to get my mind off it and onto the next book.

On the same day, I received a wire from Cliff Robertson, asking me to send a copy of the novel to him in Alicante, Spain, and a second copy to a W. Goldman in New York.

I answered him on June 8, 1964.

Dear Cliff,

Got your wire, but I'm sorry to report the book is not yet finished. I understand your impatience, but knowing how you feel about Charlie, I'm sure you wouldn't want to pressure me into sending out something unfinished. The novel changed so much since I last spoke to you that if I'd let you have it then it would have been absurdly different from what it is now—and not nearly as good.

Let me tell you that it's a lot harder to develop this thing than I thought it was going to be. I'm pleased at the progress, but I won't consider it complete until the editor who is going to see it through publication agrees with me that there is nothing further to change, develop or cut.

As soon as we're satisfied that the novel is complete, I'll send you a copy. I think you'll be pleased with the result.

People often ask if I had anything to do with the screenplay, and I tell them, "Just once."

Robertson and I continued to meet in Detroit until our last meeting before he filmed the movie. On that trip, he brought me the screenplay he had asked me to read. It was called *Good Old Charley Gordon.*

The cover page had been removed, so I had no indication who had written it.

FADE IN: was followed by a moving camera revealing an operating room scene, replete with surgeon surrounded by doctors, nurses, etc. Nurse dabs surgeon's sweating forehead. An intense, cliché operating scene. But, seconds before the credits, the camera pans in.

AND WE DISCOVER: The patient is a white mouse.

Cute, I thought, and turned the page.

The script seemed competent, well-written, clever. But I wondered why the screenwriter had changed *Alice* Kinnian to *Diane* Kinnian, or why he changed the spelling of *Charlie* to *Charley,* or why he spent so much time having M. C. Donnegan, boss of the paper box factory, looking for lemon ball candies. Minor things.

I was bothered that he had Charlie's surgery take place about *halfway through* the 133-page script. *Halfway through the movie!* And the screenwriter had stayed close to the novelette—too close, I thought. He hadn't found dramatic equivalents for the mental events of the story. He had changed the rising and falling curve structure by having Charlie deteriorate, go through a second operation, raising hopes a second time, but resulting in failure. It had the shape of a two-humped camel.

Then I remembered what Robertson had said about not wanting a downbeat ending in his feature film: "How would it be if Algernon only appears dead in the maze, and then the camera pans in, he lifts his head, wiggles his whiskers, and runs the maze?"

When I reached the last three pages, I read them with trepidation.

There it was!

Charlie is holding Algernon, *who is very much alive,* but "really very old and very tired," in his hand. Charlie raises his hand, bringing Algernon right up to his cheek. And then, A CLOSE-UP of Charlie and Algernon, cheek to cheek. A smile on Charlie's face. Tears in his eyes. And the scene fades out to the background music of "Charlie's Tune"...

Hooray for Hollywood!

I told Robertson I didn't care for the script. He said nothing and took it back.

Many years later, during a period when I harbored delusions of writing screenplays as well as novels, I bought a newly published book, *Adventures in the Screen Trade,* by a writer whose work I had long admired.

William Goldman had not only written twelve novels including *Boys and Girls Together, The Princess Bride,* and *Marathon Man,* he had also written eleven screenplays, among them *Masquerade, Harper, Butch Cassidy and the Sundance Kid, All the President's Men, Marathon Man,* and *A Bridge Too Far.*

When I opened *Adventures in the Screen Trade* and turned to the table of contents, I saw "Charly and Masquerade."

What in the world?

The chapter opens with the statement that Cliff Robertson got him into the movie business in late 1963.

Goldman points out that he had, by that time, written three novels, and was deeply blocked in his fourth when he met Robertson. He describes how Robertson told him about a story he'd optioned. Would Goldman read "Flowers for Algernon"? And if he liked it would he write the screenplay?

Goldman said yes, although he'd never written a screenplay before, and he read the story as soon as Robertson was gone. He refers to it as "a glorious piece of work."

Then, realizing that he didn't even know what a screenplay looked like, Goldman dashed down to the all-night bookstore in Times Square at two o'clock in the morning, and found a book with the word *screenwriting* in the title.

Goldman describes his meeting with Robertson in Alicante, Spain, and about returning to New York to continue on his first screenplay. After he sent the finished script to Robertson, he says, the next thing he knew he was off the project and Stirling Silliphant was writing it.

Goldman describes how shocking and painful it was for him. He'd never been fired before! Robertson hadn't even told him what was wrong with that first script he'd ever written. "But if I were forced to guess," Goldman adds, "I would say, odds on, my screenplay stunk."

Then I remembered Robertson's wire from Alicante, Spain, asking me to mail the novel to someone named Goldman in New York. I recalled the script ending with Charlie holding Algernon up to his cheek and smiling with tears in his eyes, as they go off together—that corny upbeat ending!

That's when I realized I had been, at least partially, responsible for William Goldman—one of Hollywood's A-list screenwriters—getting fired from his first movie assignment.

Sorry, Bill.

18

||||||||||||||||||||||||

WE FIND A HOME

STILL NUMB FROM THE EDITOR'S SECOND REJECTION of my novel, I set the manuscript aside until a colleague, in whom I'd confided, asked to read it. A few days later, he told me he felt the editor was mistaken. "The book is strong," he said, "but something is missing."

I winced at the double-edged comment. Maybe my mouth fell open. Maybe I blinked dumbly. I didn't know what to say. Getting out of my chair, I mumbled something like, "Well, I can't imagine what's missing, and it's too late to add anything now."

Back in my own office, I stewed over it. My colleague hadn't suggested that I make changes because of marketing needs, or editorial guesses at what readers wanted, or an ending to satisfy an audience. Going to bed that night, I thought about what he'd said. "Something is missing." He was suggesting that it needed *more of what it intended to be—something the story needed. Was there another gap I'd overlooked? What?*

Next morning I awoke with a phrase in my head: *Charlie's spiritual curve...*

And it echoed in my mind. *Where's the spiritual curve?*

Suddenly, it was clear. The original story had followed Charlie's psychological curve—intelligence, or I.Q. Then, with the love story, I'd developed his emotional curve—now sometimes called the E.Q.—or Emotional Quotient. What was missing— what Charlie still needed was the third curve, rising to the spiritual peak of his mind. Perhaps in the future it will be known as the S.Q.—or Spiritual Quotient—or just Soul Q.

I needed to find my way along the mysterious third path of Charlie's spirit.

And, so, I went back to work, thinking I must be crazy to be revising and rewriting so much. Then I remembered a passage from Sherwood Anderson's memoirs I'd often shared with writing students who protested reworking their material:

> I have seldom written a story, long or short, that I did not have to write and rewrite. There are single short stories of mine that have taken me ten or twelve years to get written.

And so it went with *Flowers for Algernon*. While my colleagues traveled to Europe during the summer of 1964, I stayed in Detroit and explored Charlie's spiritual curve. I felt it had to come after he discovers what's going to happen to him, when he knows he's going to lose it all.

And so I wrote:

> October 4—Strangest therapy session I ever had. Strauss was upset. It was something he hadn't expected either.
>
> What happened—I don't dare call it a memory—was a psychic experience or a hallucination. I won't attempt to explain or interpret it, but will only record what happened...

Although I drew on my own psychoanalytic sessions for this scene, the images and thoughts are not mine. They came out of

Charlie, who had come alive for me. As far as I was concerned, the spiritual experience in that scene was his.

I see a blue-white glow from the walls and the ceiling gathering into a shimmering ball. Now it's suspended in midair. Light...forcing itself into my eyes...and my brain...Everything in the room is aglow...I have the feeling of floating...or rather expanding up and out... and yet without looking down I know my body is still here on the couch....

Is this a hallucination?

"Charlie, are you all right?"

Or the things described by the mystics?

...I've got to ignore him. Be passive and let this—whatever it is—fill me with the light and absorb me into itself.

Charlie feels himself merging with the cosmos.

...exploding outward into the sun, I am an exploding universe swimming upward in a silent sea...And then as I know I am about to pierce the crust of existence, like a flying fish leaping out of the sea I feel the pull from below...

I wait, and leave myself open, passive to whatever this experience means. Charlie doesn't want me to pierce the upper curtain of the mind. Charlie doesn't want to know what lies beyond.

Does he fear seeing God?

Or seeing nothing.

As he reverses, and comes downward, shrinking into himself, Charlie sees the Mandala—*the multipetaled flower—swirling lotus that floats near the entrance of the unconscious.*

After the session, Strauss says, *"I think maybe that's all for today."*

"*Not only for today. I don't think I should have any more sessions. I don't want to see any more.*"

As Charlie leaves, he thinks: *And now Plato's words mock me in the shadows on the ledge behind the flames: "... the men of the cave would say of him that up he went and down he came without his eyes..."*

I hadn't planned the scene. I just let it happen and—giving part of myself, including my own break from psychoanalysis, to my fictional character—it developed far beyond a spiritual curve. It became Charlie's cosmic experience.

Two other major publishers rejected the revised novel, one on the last day of 1964:

"*... a challenging, if rather difficult, idea for a novel, which I do not feel that the author has quite managed to bring off. Its definition is clearly that of a tour de force—one character of consequence, one inevitable course—and requires, in effect, a stunning execution... I'm sorry I couldn't feel better about it.*"

Another rejection letter in March of 1965:

"*Apologies and excuses; the only reason for holding up Daniel Keyes' FLOWERS FOR ALGERNON this long... is that it caught me too, and I just had to keep it in my mind for a while.... I'll just say it is a near-miss for us, and I'm still not altogether sure I'm right to let it go, and I want very much indeed to see anything else your Mr. Keyes does, if he remains free of other publishing commitments.*"

Nice to know, but my heart grew heavier with each rejection, chipping away my ego, my determination, my hope.

The four-year lectureship agreement with Wayne State University would run out by next spring. If I didn't have a book published by then I'd have to enter a Ph.D. program to keep teaching on the college level.

For faculty teaching creative writing programs in higher education, a published book was generally considered the equivalent of a doctoral dissertation. So for me, indeed, it had become *publish* or *perish*.

I wondered if I could keep writing in the face of all this rejection. Three years of developing the novelette into a novel appeared to be going down the drain. Now, I doubted that it would ever be published. Although I hadn't written "for the drawer" as the poet Emily Dickenson had, I felt that's where my "Flowers..." would wither. No one else would ever read it.

"All right," I told myself. "Let go. It's done."

Then, as I walked along State Street toward my office at Wayne State University, something unexpected happened. I'd been short on sleep, feeling depressed, and as I neared the building, I suddenly felt an icy sweat, the blood draining from my head. I steadied myself against a streetlamp. So this was what a heart attack or a stroke was like. This was dying. This was how it all ended... My ending... The book's ending...

One last thought went through my mind before everything went black. I'm ashamed to admit that I didn't think of my wife, of my children, of the end of my world.

I said it aloud: *"Thank God I finished the novel!"*

I came to in a nearby luncheonette. I had merely fainted, and some Good Samaritan had carried me in. But, remembering what I believed to be my last words, I understood clearly what was the most important thing in my life. Not being published; not fame, or fortune or family, but finishing the book I had started.

Even if no one else ever read it, I had done it.

And I knew then, no matter what else happened to me, I would write books, and rewrite them for as long as I lived. I don't remember what I taught that day in class, but I do know I was at peace. As I had believed I was near death, I had met myself and discovered I could now call myself a novelist.

———

A month later I got a message:

Dan Wickenden of Harcourt called today to say they are
going to make an offer for *Flowers for Algernon*.

I didn't believe it. But then I received his note. "I can now officially bid you welcome to Harcourt, Brace & World, Inc., and
say how pleased I am to be the editor of such an original, fascinating, and affecting first novel."

What most struggling writers go through. From despair to exultation, from the depths to the heights, from tears to laughter—turned me around so quickly I became dizzy, and fearful
that acceptance was a dream that would fade with morning light.

But it wasn't a dream.

The contract called for September 1, 1965, as the delivery
date for my final revisions of the manuscript.

Revisions?

Of course. I didn't mind revising, as long as...

Wickenden asked for some cutting. He wrote: "The early,
pre-operation Progress Reports, and those immediately following the operation, are something of an obstacle partly because of
the spelling and grammar, partly because... when the results of
the operation begin to show clearly, they are essentially exposi-
tory... If the 38 pages could be reduced to, say, 28 pages, it
might be all to the good."

Cut ten pages? No problem there.

He suggested one other change: "How would you feel about
placing Charlie's excursion to Warren earlier in the book, sending
him out there before he knows for sure that is where he'll wind up?
I think the Warren episode would fit in quite easily following page
236, which comes after Charlie's question about being able to in-
spect the place."

When I glanced through the manuscript, I was stunned.

The place to which Dan Wickenden suggested I move the episode *was where I had originally written it.* I'd shifted it to a later point for some reason I now forget. But I was amazed at this editor's perception. I attributed his sensitivity to the fact that he too had been a novelist.

"Bear in mind," he added, "that all my suggestions are only suggestions, and if any or all of them strike you as being wrong-headed, so be it. It is your book, and we don't want you to do anything that goes against the grain."

Algernon and Charlie and I had finally found a home.

PART FIVE

||||||||||||||||||||||

Post-Publication Blues

19

||||||||||||||||||||||

"Don't Hide Your Light Under a Bushel"

I THOUGHT I WAS HOME FREE. I believed that acceptance of a book manuscript by a publisher was the reward at the end of the maze, and the writer could bask in glory. I was wrong again. A writer faces many false turns and dead ends. Moments of exultation shatter into months of despair.

In my files, I have an acknowledgment of my returning the $650 and cancellation of the contract with the first publisher. But I also learned that the Harcourt advance wouldn't be mine until the manuscript had been editorially accepted, as well as legally accepted. That meant it had to be cleared by attorneys who examined it for libel, copyright infringement, and other small print legal problems. If they considered the book unpublishable, I would have to return their advance as well.

There was much more work to do. The publicity department needed an autobiographical sketch, and names of well-known authors who knew me well enough to read an advance copy and say things that might be used in a blurb as a quote to praise the novel. The very thought embarrassed me, and still does.

I was also asked for names of "opinion makers" or celebrities I knew, who might spread the all-important word of mouth or, as one reviewer later quipped about Algernon, "...he got good word-of-mouse."

The only one I knew was a colleague in the Journalism Department at Wayne State University who reviewed books for the *Detroit News*. We talked, and he assured me that if my editor sent him an advance copy, he would review my novel.

Well, it was a start.

What happened next? I got galley proofs—my last chance to make changes before page proofs. Too many changes and I'd have to pay for them. But I wanted my work to go out into the world with as few mistakes as possible.

At this point, I learned that bound proofs, with the notation "Uncorrected Galleys," had been sent to the powerful prepublication reviewers, *Virginia Kirkus Bulletin, Library Journal,* and *Publishers Weekly,* who needed them about three months before publication day. These reviews would influence libraries, independent bookstores, and major book chains. They might also affect newspaper and magazine reviewers whose columns were usually held until *after* the official publication date when books would be in the stores. So prepublication reviews were the first ones anyone saw and often set the tone for those that followed.

The first hint that something was wrong came about two months before publication day. My acquaintance from the Department of Journalism stopped me in the corridor. "Dan, your publisher sent me bound galleys of *Flowers for Algernon*. I haven't read it yet, but I've decided it's not right for me—as a colleague of yours—to review it. I've passed it along to my friend Phil Thomas on the Associated Press staff. He's a short story writer, and he's agreed to read it."

I thanked him but went back to my office with a sinking feeling that something was wrong. What could have turned him around? I went to the periodicals section of the library and asked for the most recent *Virginia Kirkus Bulletin*. She handed me the issue dated January 1, 1966. And there it was.

FLOWERS FOR ALGERNON

For lovers of Science Fiction, this story, in its original form was always a special kind of tour de force, a classic to be given to people you were trying to convert to the genre. Now, and regretfully, unfortunately, it has been turned into a full novel which in turn is being made into a motion picture. The idea is still unique...But now, oh what Freudian psychoses riddle the pages...What shapely Hollywooden scenes come to view. What bastardization of what was once so beautifully put...

I dashed into the men's room and threw up. And then I wandered through that day with the deepest depression I had ever known. I understood now why my colleague didn't want to review it. He had obviously checked out *Kirkus*. And the *Kirkus* reviewer—the very first reviewer—had fulfilled my earliest fears. How dare I tamper with a *classic* story? Six years of work from novelette to novel had resulted in the epithet—bastardization!

I remember every moment of that despair, not only with my brain but in my gut. It still hurts. But, enough. Let it go.

I had to wait three weeks for the second prepublication review. *Publishers Weekly* said, "*FLOWERS FOR ALGERNON* is a strikingly original first novel..."

Praise also in the *Library Journal:* "This is an absorbing first novel, immensely original, which is going to be read for a long time to come...Purchase in duplicate is recommended."

The *New York Times* published a full-length review in the midweek "Books of the Times" by Eliot Fremont-Smith, a respected literary reviewer. Here's the beginning and the end of his review:

THE MESSAGE AND THE MAZE

Algernon is a mouse and the flowers are for his grave, which explains the innervating title of this novel but does not convey Daniel Keyes's love of problems... [It] is a technician's maze, a collection of nasty little challenges for a writer of fiction. That it works at all as a novel is proof of Mr. Keyes's deftness. And it is really quite a performance...a tale that is convincing, suspenseful and touching—all in a modest degree, but it is enough...The skill shown here is awesome... Mr. Keyes runs his maze at least as well as Algernon and Charlie run theirs, which is exciting in itself...And affecting too...how otherwise explain the tears that come to one's eyes at the novel's end?

I was dizzy. I read it again and again. Tears came to my eyes. I choke up even now, thinking about it.

Thank you, Mr. Eliot Fremont-Smith, wherever you are.

The novel has since had hundreds of reviews, all positive. Only that first—the *Virginia Kirkus Bulletin*—was negative. Why does it still hurt? I want to forget that first pain of novel-birth.

But it is not a bastardization!

Well, maybe my reliving it now will get it out of my system or, at least, numb the pain.

Of course, I should have known better than to care. I know better now, but knowing is different from feeling. From time to time, I share with my students Turgenev's thoughts on "Public Approval and Reward."

Poet, set no store by popular applause. The moment of extravagant praise will pass, and you will hear about you the judgements of fools and the laughter of the cold multitude. But do you stand firm, calm and undaunted.

You are a king and, as such, just live in loneliness. Tread

freely where the spirit of freedom leads, endlessly perfecting the fruit of your chosen thoughts, and seeking no rewards for noble deeds.

Your work is its own reward: you are the supreme judge of what you have accomplished. With greater severity than anybody else you can determine its value.

Are you content? If so, you can afford to ignore the condemnation of the crowd.

Easier said than done. I can almost sense the pain and disappointment behind those words. Turgenev, I suspect, must have gotten some lousy reviews.

On the same day as the *New York Times* review, Cliff Robertson called to tell me he'd just finished taping an interview for the *Merv Griffin Show*, displaying the novel and announcing his forthcoming movie version.

The *Merv Griffin Show* didn't air in Detroit until three weeks later. By coincidence, on the same day, the *Detroit News* published a favorable review by my colleague's friend, Phil Thomas, that began: "Charlie Gordon will break your heart."

What more could a writer ask for?

Only one thing.

Proud papa that I was, I went to the book section of Hudson's main department store in downtown Detroit, and tried to appear nonchalant as I sauntered through the book section looking for *Flowers for Algernon*.

Not a single copy.

When I introduced myself to the book buyer, he seemed surprised that the salesman had never mentioned it. He would order some copies, but now that the publicity had passed, he said, it wouldn't do much good.

When my friends and colleagues phoned to say they couldn't

find copies of the book, I started calling stores. That sinking feeling again. Except for the Doubleday Bookshop in the Fisher Building, which had promptly sold out its stock of three copies, none of the other bookstores had ordered a single copy. Their managers all said they were annoyed that they hadn't been alerted to a "local" author.

I complained to my editor, "What good are reviews and publicity if there are no books in the stores?"

I'll never forget Dan Wickenden's response, and I pass it on to other writers as a cautionary tale.

"Dan, you don't mean to tell me that you didn't get in touch with the bookstores in Detroit and tell them about it."

"No," I said. "I'm kind of shy. And I didn't think it was my job."

"Dan, you shouldn't hide your light under a bushel."

For what it's worth, let me point out that ever since—wherever I travel—I talk to booksellers. If they have copies of my books, I ask if they would like me to sign them. They usually do, and then affix stickers to the cover, saying: AUTOGRAPHED. It helps sell books, and they rarely return them to the publisher. Experience toughens us.

20

‖‖‖‖‖‖‖‖‖‖‖‖‖‖‖‖‖‖‖‖

WHEN ARE WRITERS
LIKE SAINTS?

PUBLICATION OF THE NOVEL in the spring of 1966 encouraged me to search for a tenure-track teaching position. Again, I sent letters to universities across the country, but this time I got *three* requests for job interviews. One, from Ohio University in Athens, Ohio, looked promising.

When I met Professor Edgar Whan, chairman of the English Department, he said, "I've read *Flowers for Algernon*. It's a fine novel. We're offering you a position of lecturer like the others in our Creative Writing Program. That enables the department to bring you in on the pay scale and academic level of professor instead of assistant professor. You'll get a formal letter in a few days, but I wanted to let you know right away."

"I appreciate that."

"You know," he said, "I've always believed that creative writing should be taught by working writers, professionals—not aesthetes or critics. But I've observed that most English Departments feel about writers the way the Church feels about saints."

"How's that?"

"They'd prefer not to have them around until after they're dead."

I accepted the job.

Aurea and I and our daughters, Hillary and Leslie, moved to Athens, Ohio, in the summer of 1966. I was to start teaching in the fall.

The day after I arrived, I got a phone call from Walter Tevis, author of *The Hustler*, welcoming me to Athens. He'd been hired for the writing program the previous year.

We met in a downtown restaurant, and shared thoughts about writing and the writer's life. Tevis said, though he'd been born in Kentucky he'd always dreamed of being a New York writer, of being in the center of the literary scene. He talked about his short stories, sold to the "slicks"—magazines printed on coated paper, and a cut above the rough "pulps" I had worked on. He talked about *The Hustler*, published by Harper's in 1959, and the successful movie with Paul Newman and Jackie Gleason.

He sounded bitter, however, that Harper's had rejected his second novel, *The Man Who Fell to Earth*, and that he'd eventually had to sell it as a paperback original. He'd had a writer's block ever since, he said—hadn't written a thing—even though the novel later became a highly praised science fiction movie starring David Bowie.

He told me about the other writers in the program. They were away for the summer, but I'd meet them in a few weeks: the poet Hollis Summers, the novelist and short story writer Jack Matthews, and the nonfiction writer Norman Schmidt.

"Norm's no kid," he said. "He's published a couple of novels under the pseudonym *James Norman*. He was a reporter for American newspapers in Europe during the 1930s, and a newscaster for the Spanish republican government. He even knew Hemingway during the Spanish civil war."

I thanked Tevis for his warm welcome. I had never before been in a position to talk about the writing and publishing life with another mainstream novelist. I had often imagined myself in Paris in the 1920s among the expatriate authors in the cafés of Montmartre, sharing the literary life. This was the closest I would come—in Athens, Ohio, in 1966. But I knew I would enjoy living and teaching and writing close to other working writers.

That evening, as I played with my daughters in our new home, I found myself whistling "When the Saints Go Marching In."

21

||||||||||||||||||||||||

CHARLY GOES HOLLYWOOD

FLOWERS FOR ALGERNON SOLD OUT its 5,000 copy first printing in a few days, and Harcourt rushed out another 1,000 copies, and then reprinted 1,000 at a time. Still, from 1966 until now, it has never gone out of print in hardcovers, and was reissued in the Harcourt Brace Modern Classics Series.

The Science Fiction Writers of America voted the novel a Nebula Award trophy, in a tie for "Best Novel 1966," and Bantam Books bought the reprint rights for mass-market paperback publication.

In the meantime, I applied to two writers' colonies for residence fellowships the following summer to work on my radiation novel and was accepted by both. I spent the first two months at Yaddo in Saratoga Springs, New York, and the third month at "The MacDowell Colony" in Peterborough, New Hampshire.

On my second or third morning at Yaddo, a young writer whose first novel was about to be published came down to breakfast looking distraught. I heard him mumbling into his coffee a couple of times, and only on the third mumble did I hear his words.

"Virginia Kirkus says I wrote 'a scabrous novel'..."

Remembering my own reaction to my *Kirkus* review, I said something like, "Don't pay any attention. Don't let it get to you." But I don't think he heard me. He just kept mumbling over and over, "Kirkus says I wrote 'a scabrous novel.'"

That young writer was Robert Stone, whose first novel *Hall of Mirrors* was made into the movie *WUSA* starring Paul Newman and Joanne Woodward. Later, Stone won the National Book Award for his 1975 novel, *Dog Soldiers,* and was among the finalists in 1982 and 1992. In 1998 he was a finalist for *Damascus Gate.* Whenever I hear his work praised, I recall his plaintive cry about his first book, "Kirkus says I wrote 'a scabrous novel.'"

At Yaddo, I continued working on my second novel about the young couple contaminated by radiation. I finished it later that summer at the MacDowell Colony. Harcourt Brace accepted it and scheduled it for publication as *The Touch* the following year.

And what about Cliff Robertson's movie? Many celebrated writers have protested that their work has been destroyed on the screen. The common notion, as far as Hollywood is concerned, is that the book's author is the last one they want around after contracts are signed. The only way for the writer to avoid heartbreak, they say, is, "Take the money and run."

But I could never feel that way about Algernon and Charlie. I cared deeply about what might happen to them on the big screen, and I was worried about what Robertson might have done to the ending. After I had given him my negative opinion of the William Goldman screenplay, I heard nothing more from Robertson for another year.

Shortly after Bantam published the paperback edition of *Flowers for Algernon,* Cliff Robertson visited Ohio University to be honored by the Aeronautical Program. He piloted his small plane into the Athens airport, and cameras flashed as he opened the cockpit and climbed down. When he saw me, he smiled. "Dan, you're going to be proud of me when you see *Charly.* We kept your downbeat ending."

I remembered his plan for Algernon to wiggle his whiskers and run the maze at the end to show he was still alive, but I said nothing.

His visit was, of course, a photo opportunity, and the *Athens Messenger* and Ohio University's student newspaper, *The Post,* had been alerted for pictures and interviews. The Biology Department provided a white mouse as a stand-in, and photographers took pictures of Robertson holding an Algernon look-alike as I show them both a copy of the new movie tie-in paperback with him and Claire Bloom on the cover.

The following morning, Robertson and I had breakfast together at his hotel. He talked about the film. As coproducer, he said proudly, he'd assumed major creative control. He'd sent director Ralph Nelson to Canada to learn the new movie techniques of EXPO-67, and then insisted on a modern look with split-screen projection and multiple images. The musical sound track was composed and played by Ravi Shankar featuring his sitar, and using both exotic and conventional strings as well as ancient and modern woodwinds.

He said, only one thing bothered him. As he had told me years earlier at the Detroit Airport, he had never intended for Algernon to die at the end. But in the film's convention scene, when Charlie holds the mouse in his hand, Algernon looks dead. Robertson said before the film's release, he'd phoned director Ralph Nelson, who was in London at the time, and told him to shoot a close-up of a hand—any hand—holding a live white mouse wiggling its whiskers, so they could splice it during the final edit.

"But yesterday, you said you kept the downbeat ending."

He shrugged. "Ralph never got to shoot that close-up."

The International Berlin Film Festival selected *Charly* as the "American Entry of 1968," and in the fall it premiered in New York. I stood across the street from the Baronet Theater, watching the line of moviegoers that snaked around the corner.

After a deep breath of Broadway air, I crossed the street to get in line, and bought my ticket. Inside, after the lights dimmed, I heard the twanging music of Ravi Shankar's sitar, saw childlike Charlie on the playground swing, and then lost myself in the movie of my "What would happen if...?"

I felt a twinge of disappointment that they'd changed the setting to Boston, instead of New York City, the place of memories I had given to Charlie.

Charly received rave reviews. *The Long Island Press* reviewer called it "Dynamic," with "...a chilling ending that speaks volumes."

So the original downbeat ending had made it intact to the screen, and people around the world would see it as I'd written it.

The film's first award came from *Scholastic Magazine,* which had published the "Flowers for Algernon" novelette version several times, in 1961, 1963, 1964, 1965, and 1967. *Scholastic* gave *Charly* the Bell Ringer Award in 1968, as the "Best Movie of the Year."

Someone at Bantam must have realized the potential for the use of the novel in education, because they launched a FLOWERS FOR ALGERNON—CHARLY—BANTAM BOOKS/CINERAMA JOINT PROMOTION pilot project. The plan was to sponsor a series of preview screenings for educators in key cities where the movie was to be shown.

At the first screening in Chicago, each of the 450 teachers

who attended was given a kit containing a copy of the paperback novel, a study guide for teaching it, and an interview between Ralph Nelson, the film's producer/director, and Stirling Silliphant, the screenwriter, discussing their creative collaboration.

Cliff Robertson put in a personal appearance, and was greeted by a wildly enthusiastic audience and a standing ovation. He conducted a symposium following the movie. The next day he did the same thing in Milwaukee at a special screening for the National Council of Teachers of English.

In New York and Los Angeles, where *Charly* had already opened, teachers were invited to the movie during its regular playing schedule. Although New York teachers were on strike, more than five hundred teachers from private and parochial schools attended screenings and received copies of the teachers' kit.

Bantam and Cinerama arranged preview screenings in other major cities throughout the country, and more than 25,000 English teachers and their families saw the movie and received free copies of the novel. The director of sales wrote to keep me up to date: "The interest and activity are gaining tremendous momentum."

Hollywood buzzed that Cliff Robertson would be nominated for an Academy Award as Best Actor.

He was and he won.

I am often asked, as are most writers whose work has been transformed into a film, "What did you think of the movie?" It's awkward to answer that without seeming petty or ungrateful. But then a postgraduate student from another university, doing his thesis on "Adaptation of Literature for the Screen," asked about my reaction to the movie version.

I wrote back that I understood changes had been needed to translate the story to film. Some of these enhanced the work, by adding to or intensifying it. For example: In the novel, when Charlie is frustrated at one stage of his growth, he goes on a movie binge in Times Square—as I used to do. The film version in Boston has him go on a midget-auto bumper cars binge on a midway. Much more visual. The idea of frustration is well-handled, and yet nothing is lost or harmed.

And when genius Charlie sees himself as the earlier Charlie— during a nightmare pursuit through a maze of hotel corridors— it's imaginative and well done. The scene complements passages in the book, in which genius Charlie discovers the first Charlie is still within him.

But there are added sections, techniques, and scenes which I feel are unnecessary, and which detract from the story. As Charlie and Alice develop a relationship, they're shown in a slow-motion romp through the woods. It looks like a shampoo or deodorant TV commercial.

The scene in which Charlie forces his attention on Alice and then becomes a motorcycle-gang, black-leather-jacket, drug-cult member violates his character. One of my points in the novel is that his basic personality doesn't change with a change of intelligence. He is still Charlie.

These changes were obviously made for commercial reasons, as were the trendy film techniques: zoom camera angles, and split and multiple screens. One reviewer pointed out that these might have been needed to maintain interest in a film with a less compelling story line, but they weren't necessary for *Charly.*

Life Magazine's reviewer wrote, "The best scenes, like those in which Charlie competes with the mouse in getting through a maze, are straight from the book. The worst, like the medical convention where he tells off the doctors, were invented for the movie."

I think the film suffers when it avoids the denouement, and makes a quick jump from Charlie's discovery of what is going to happen to him to a sudden frozen-faced ending on the swing in the schoolyard. Robertson had warned me earlier that he felt the audience wouldn't be able to tolerate the agony of the downward curve of Charlie's deterioration. But I believe this is the major power and structure of both the novelette and the novel. Charlie's tragic fall should have been shown.

I don't insist that filmmakers are obliged to adhere to the original story, but I do think that changes should preserve the integrity of the work, rather than modify it for strictly commercial reasons.

As for Cliff Robertson's portrayal of Charlie, I feel he deserved the Oscar he won.

But I have to admit I'm glad director Ralph Nelson didn't find a mouse in London that could wiggle its whiskers.

22

||||||||||||||||||||||||

BROADWAY BOUND

SEVEN YEARS AFTER the movie was released, I received a letter from David Rogers, who had written a play version of *Flowers for Algernon* for nonprofessional theater, saying he and a composer were interested in doing a first-class dramatic-musical version for the stage. I was fascinated by the thought. Musical theater was the only medium in which the story had not yet appeared.

Rogers had presented the idea to Charles Strouse, composer of such hit shows as *Bye-Bye Birdie, Golden Boy,* and *Applause.* His latest, *Annie,* was soon to open, and Strouse was eager to write the music for *Flowers for Algernon.*

The amateur theatrical version had been performed successfully for seven years in high schools and in stock groups around the country, and now the Dramatic Publishing Company was prepared to help finance the musical. The producer planned to open the show in late 1977 or early 1978.

I reminded them that I would have to submit their offer to Cliff Robertson under his "right of first refusal," but they felt certain that, since he could have no interest in doing a stage musical, there surely would be no problem.

They were wrong.

After receiving the offer of "first refusal" Robertson contested my right to make the deal. It took the next three years to bring the case to arbitration in Los Angeles.

In the meantime, among the hundreds of letters from readers about *Flowers for Algernon,* one from a psychiatrist led me to a new path for my next two books.

She wrote that she and her colleague were doing research into literary examples of "autoscopy," now sometimes referred to as the out-of-body experience. They had noticed its frequent occurrence in *Flowers for Algernon.*

I knew what she was referring to, but I hadn't recalled that it had appeared *frequently.* Rereading the novel, I was surprised.

After Charlie becomes a genius, he often *sees* the other Charlie. When he and Alice are at the concert in Central Park, and he puts his arms around her, he believes he sees a boy watching them.

||||||||||||||||

All the way back to her apartment, it was on my mind that the boy had been crouching there in the darkness, and for one second I had caught a glimpse of what he was seeing—the two of us lying in each other's arms. *(Harcourt paperback edition, page 101)*

||||||||||||||||

Somehow, getting drunk had momentarily broken down the conscious barriers that kept the old Charlie Gordon hidden deep in my mind. As I suspected all along, he was not really gone. Nothing in our minds is ever really gone. The operation had covered him over with a veneer of education and culture, but emotionally he was there—watching and waiting. *(page 195)*

||||||||||||||||

"I can't help feeling that I'm not me. I've usurped his place and I locked him out the way they locked me out of the bakery... I've discovered that not only did Charlie exist in the past, he exists now. In me and around me..." (*page 201*)

IIIIIIIIIIIIIIII

For one moment I had the cold feeling he was watching. Over the arm of the couch, I caught a glimpse of his face staring back at me through the dark beyond the window—where just a few minutes earlier I had been crouching. A switch in perception, and I was out on the fire escape again, watching a man and a woman inside making love on the couch.

Then, with a violent effort of the will, I was back on the couch with her... and I saw the face against the window, hungrily watching. And I thought to myself, go ahead, you poor bastard—watch. I don't give a damn any more.

And his eyes went wide as he watched. (*page 209*)

IIIIIIIIIIIIIIII

The psychiatrist's letter pointed out that authors in whose work autoscopy appeared seemed to fall into one of two categories: For some writers, like E. T. A. Hoffman, it revealed a symptom of mental disorder. For other writers, it was merely a literary device. She wanted to know in which category I belonged. I wrote back that I had never had these experiences, except as a conscious act of the imagination. As far as I was concerned, Charlie's *self-seeing* is a literary device.

Then, fascinated that this phenomenon appeared so often in my book, I began to study the psychiatric literature on autoscopy and related subjects. Out-of-body experiences led me to doppelgängers, doubles, alter egos, dual personalities, and finally multiple personality disorder (MPD), now called dissociative identity disorder (DID).

I read several short novelettes in which the double appears: Poe's "William Wilson," Dostoyevsky's "The Double," and Conrad's "The Secret Sharer."

And, of course, there were the two famous nonfiction case histories: *The Three Faces of Eve* and *Sybil*. But it occurred to me that no one had ever written a full-length novel dealing with this aspect of the multiple personality disorder.

The psychiatrist's comments about Genius Charlie seeing the First Charlie began to germinate into my third novel—*The Fifth Sally*—a story about a mind in conflict with itself. That letter had been another "given."

Shortly afterward, I flew to Los Angeles to face Cliff Robertson during two days of testimony. Several weeks later I received the award of arbitration.

"CLAIMANT, Daniel Keyes, under the reservation of rights provision of the contract of August 18, 1961 is free to convey to the offeree the stage rights in the dramatic-musical version of CLAIMANT'S work 'Flowers for Algernon.'"

So, while I was working on *The Fifth Sally*, my experimental novel, a singing Charlie and a dancing white mouse were rehearsing for the musical stage.

Let me describe briefly what I heard on the first audiotape Rogers and Strouse sent me. The show's opening number is a childlike melody with simple lyrics: "I got a friend today, someone to laugh and play. I got a friend."

As Charlie's intelligence improves, the songs become increasingly complex, sophisticated. At the high point he sings an operatic aria—"Charlie." Then, as his intelligence deteriorates, his songs become simpler, until it ends with a plaintive rock number. *"I really loved ya—"*

They had done, in lyrics and music, the equivalent of the story's spelling and sentence structure—showing Charlie's rise and fall by the way he communicates.

It is a one-act production. No chance of anyone "second acting." At the end, Charlie sits sadly by Algernon's grave in the backyard.

Because of the complex arbitration over the dramatic-musical rights, the show's opening was delayed. Since one of Charles Strouse's other musicals was having problems during its out-of-town engagement in Washington, D.C., he transferred one of Charlie's major songs to the new show.

"Tomorrow" helped make *Annie* a hit.

I couldn't get to the first out-of-town performances at the Citadel Theatre in Edmonton, Canada, but the producers sent me the glowing notices.

I saw the show for the first time on opening night at the Queen's Theatre in London's West End—the British equivalent of Broadway. A young popular British actor I had never heard of before played the singing, dancing Charlie.

I watched, entranced as he carried the mood from the sad memories of his parents' suffering to the comic turn as he and the white mouse dance across the stage as a vaudeville duo. At one point, Algernon cavorts across Charlie's black turtleneck sweater, and then, in a soft-shoe number, under twin spotlights, Charlie dances, while Algernon runs in circles beside him. A showstopper.

The London production drew good notices, but there had been a cloud over it from the beginning. Opening week coincided with the British government's start of the Value Added Tax—a hefty tax surcharge on almost all products. Londoners were buying refrigerators, washing machines, and cars before the V.A.T. sent prices soaring. They weren't buying theater tickets.

As the *Wall Street Journal* wrote: "The London theater...is in deep financial trouble...the recent near-doubling of the national sales tax, known as value added tax or VAT, is forcing higher ticket prices and driving away new audiences. West End producers and actors were recently shocked by the closing of two productions everyone expected to be hits. 'Flowers for Algernon,'...lasted only 29 performances."

I was on a driving tour through England with my family, when the closing notice reached us in Oxford. We returned to London in time for the cast farewell party as the set was struck—drinks in paper cups, sad good-byes.

Years later, when I visited the young actor backstage, in his dressing room in New York, he told me that after Andrew Lloyd Webber had seen him singing and dancing with Algernon in London, he offered him the lead in his new show.

Annie had gotten Charlie's song, "Tomorrow."

And our singing, dancing Charlie—Michael Crawford—had become "Phantom of the Opera."

The producers still had their hearts set on Broadway. The new American production of *Flowers for Algernon* was renamed *Charlie and Algernon,* subtitled, "A Very Special Musical." Sponsored by the Kennedy Center, the Fisher Theater Foundation, Isobel Robins Konecky, and the Folger Theater Group, the show had its out-of-town tryout in Washington, D.C.

Charlie was performed by P. J. Benjamin, who dedicated his performance to his sister, and "to all the other special people in this world."

The Washington limited engagement received fine notices, and, after a brief standing-room-only run at the intimate Terrace

Theater, it made a "Return Engagement by Popular Demand" to the 1,500-seat Eisenhower Theater.

Mel Gusso reviewed the Kennedy Center production for the *New York Times:*

> This seemingly unlikely musical material... becomes the basis of a show with a heart about our minds... [during] the title song, a cheerfully sardonic vaudeville turn about [Charlie's] disillusionment, he places the mouse on stage in a spotlight, and on cue—do our eyes deceive us?—the mouse appears to dance to the music. This rousing tune is immediately followed by "The Maze," a Jacques Brel-like swirling carousel of a song about Charlie's labyrinthine confusion.... Algernon is in a class by himself. This is one mouse that earns its cheese.

After a review like that, the show moved to Broadway's Helen Hayes Theater in New York with high expectations.

The first hint of trouble surfaced when the producers learned that David Merrick's musical, *42nd Street,* based on the 1933 hit movie, would be opening the same night. An extravaganza, with massive advertising and promotion, was pitted against our small show.

But there was hope. As one columnist put it, "*Charlie and Algernon*... whose high spot is a 'dance' with a man and mouse, is getting good 'word of mouse' talk."

In the *Playbill*'s "Who's Who in the Cast," Algernon is listed as being played by *Himself,* and having had "extensive training in jazz, tap and mazerunning." Although Algernon is quoted as applauding the title, "He would have preferred alphabetical billing."

So *Charlie and Algernon* made it to Broadway. I sat proudly in the orchestra with family, relatives, and friends, as the house lights dimmed and the curtain rose to Charlie's childlike tune....

The musical numbers build in complexity. "The Maze" is followed by "Whatever Time There Is," a plaintive love duet between Charlie and Alice, foreshadowing the ending.

In an operatic aria at the peak of his intelligence, "Charlie" soars to heights I had never imagined. Hearing it, I find myself almost hoping they had changed the ending at the last moment. Like the rest of the audience, I don't want Charlie to lose it all, and I don't want Algernon to die.

But Charlie's simple, final song, "I Really Loved You," surprises tears from my eyes.

As Charlie sits beside Algernon's grave, the theater is silent. When the curtain falls, there is an explosion of applause. Charlie brings Algernon back on stage to take his bow. At the drum roll, Algernon runs a little circle.

A roar from the audience and a standing ovation.

There is no way to convey the excitement of an opening night at the theater, especially if the characters and story are your own creation. As the audience leaves, buzzing with praise for the show, the rest of us head for the traditional opening-night party at Sardi's.

The gathering includes the producers, backers, cast, friends, columnists, and theater people—the "glitterati," as someone once dubbed them. This is the feast before the high point, the ritual of waiting for tomorrow's *New York Times* review, which will hit the stands by eleven o'clock tonight. We have no worries about that. Hadn't Mel Gusso, reviewing it for the *Times,* already praised it in Washington, as "...a show with a heart about our minds"?

As we enter Sardi's I recall my visit to the men's room after my adolescent "second acting" opening-night debacle. The situation has changed, and I'm happy to be back in New York. Sardi's is my dream come true.

But after a while, I sense something. A chill in the air. People drifting toward the exit. What's going on? Then I see people in the anteroom reading newspapers. The *New York Times* has arrived. I feel a tightness in my chest. Someone hands me a copy, and I read the review by Frank Rich.

"Though this musical boasts unusual heroes and enough philosophical truisms to fill a dozen fortune cookies, it is a very ordinary and at times very irritating entertainment."

David Rogers's book and lyrics comes in for harsh criticism. *"...Mr. Rogers exploits his brain-damaged hero for ready-made bathos...The tone of the evening is not so much inspirational as manipulative and smug"..."old fashioned direction, [and the] minimal choreography do not exactly send the evening's fractionalized components into orbit."*

Frank Rich calls Charles Strouse's music, *"often tuneful but rarely rousing."* Unaware that "Tomorrow" had originally been written for Charlie, Rich complains: *"Indeed, there are a number of songs that baldly attempt to repackage the uplift of 'Tomorrow' from Mr. Strouse's 'Annie.'"*

Mr. Rich refers to the set as, *"drably utilitarian."*

He praises only P. J. Benjamin: *"Once Charlie gains his faculties, the attractive Mr. Benjamin displays a sweet voice and limber charm that are the show's principal assets."* But the actress who plays Alice *"is hamstrung by a wan singing voice."*

Rich adds, *"Of course, I'm not forgetting about Algernon. He's a cute little mouse...and he does a mean little softshoe. Still, I must confess that even his tragic death, just in time for the final curtain, left me cold."*

"...'Charlie and Algernon' pays far too cheap a price for its audience's tears."

By the time my guests and I leave Sardi's, the place is almost empty. No one speaks. A pall of death hangs over the dining room as waiters clear the tables still laden with food and drink. The producers keep the show open for thirty days. *Charlie and Algernon* is nominated for a Tony Award, for Best Musical Score, too late to save it. I feel Frank Rich has already killed it. And Algernon's death, he says, "left him cold."

Well, what do I expect? I'd fought for the tragic ending. I can't complain. A line from the last song flows through my mind. *"It's really over..."*

But, of course, it never is.

23

||||||||||||||||||||||||

AND THEN WHAT HAPPENED?

THROUGHOUT THE '70S, '80S, AND '90S, as I wrote and published several other books, TV producers contacted me directly and through various agents about licensing the rights to make "Flowers for Algernon" into a movie for television. I had believed all those years, since 1961, when I signed Cliff Robertson's movie contract, that I had reserved those rights for myself.

Everywhere the legal language included the words *TV rights,* I had insisted they be crossed out. Robertson had bought the movie rights for what I believed was a pittance when I was a young, inexperienced author, and even at that time I'd felt the agents and attorneys were giving away too much for too little.

So I had insisted on retaining TV movie rights.

However, several prominent entertainment attorneys agreed with Cliff Robertson that I did not own TV movie rights, because, they said, when I had signed the contract, "Made for TV Movies," or "Movies of the Week" did not exist. Therefore, according to industry custom, *I must have meant* I was reserving only *live TV movie rights.*

And, they insisted, no one was doing live TV movies.

When I received an offer for the television motion picture rights from Citadel Entertainment, I submitted it to Cliff Robertson again under "the right of first refusal" clause. Through his attorney, he insisted he already owned those rights, and I could not license them to anyone else.

Three years later, with Citadel's help, I went back to Beverly Hills—back to arbitration. Then, ten years after the previous arbitration over the dramatic-musical, I received the news:

AWARD OF ARBITRATOR

Claimant is entitled to develop, license and otherwise exploit his book "Flowers for Algernon" for a television movie pursuant to an agreement with Citadel Entertainment.

David Ginsberg, president of Citadel, told the *Hollywood Reporter:* "From the lawyer's side of my brain I believed... profoundly that we could legally secure these rights. The creative side of my brain wanted to do this project so much that it was worth the years of litigation to have it finally concluded in our favor."

A new TV two-hour movie, keeping the original title, was then scheduled to be telecast by CBS-TV as a "major event" movie during the February 2000 "sweeps." The script, written by John Pielmeier, who wrote *Agnes of God,* pleased me. Matthew Modine, an actor I had admired ever since I saw him in *Birdy,* was cast as Charlie. Principal photography was begun in April 1999—exactly forty years after first publication of the novelette in *The Magazine of Fantasy and Science Fiction.*

The novel version never made any of the bestseller lists, because its sales have been spread over more than thirty-four years. Yet, slowly, it has made its own way around the world. To put things in perspective: Bantam Books has sold almost five million copies of the paperback edition. It is taught in schools at all levels across the country.

In Japan, sales by Hayakawa Publishing have now reached a million and a half copies in hardcovers. It is used in Japanese schools, in both English and Japanese, to teach students how to read and write English.

Since its first publication, the novel version has been published in twenty-seven foreign editions.

Over the past forty years, I've been asked two recurring questions. First, "Why do you write? And why did you write this particular story?"

I remember the late Walter Tevis once telling me he'd written *The Hustler, The Man Who Fell to Earth,* and *The Color of Money,* "... for fame, fortune, and the love of beautiful women." I knew that wasn't why I wrote, and I've never had an easy answer for that question. Perhaps that's why I've written this memoir, as my own "summing up."

Recently, I was given another unexpected gift that connected me to the past, and gave me the answer to *why* I'd become a writer.

On the morning that seventy-seven-year-old John Glenn, the *Challenger* crew, and NASA were preparing for the shuttle's return to earth, I was preparing to deliver the keynote address for the Seventeenth Annual Writers Conference of the Space Coast Writers Guild a few miles away, in Cocoa Beach, Florida.

I had struggled the night before to find an ending to the talk, but I was frustrated and unsatisfied. At breakfast the next morning, I was handed a bulky manila envelope. There was no explanatory note—just a sheaf of about thirty letters from students describing their reactions after having read the novelette version of "Flowers for Algernon."

Later, I learned they had been written by graduating ninth-grade junior high school students in two gifted classes as part of a class assignment competition. I was deeply touched. Writers of the three winning letters, selected by their classmates, had

been awarded an all-expense-paid visit to the conference to sit
with me.

I didn't plan what was to follow. As I reached the end of my
address, thinking about "why" I wrote, I recalled Tevis's comment about writing for "fame, fortune, and the love of beautiful
women," and I quoted it. Then I read aloud passages from the
award-winning student letters I had been given that morning.

Dear Mr. Keyes,

With the example of Charlie Gordon's thirst for knowledge, I too wanted to grasp all the knowledge I could. This
story very quickly became my favorite.

Wanting to share this story with others, I read the story
over the phone to my friend.... He listened intently, never
saying a word. Personally, I thought he fell asleep. After reading the last few words... I asked why he was so silent. Snif-
fling, with a soft voice he replied, "That's the most touching
story I've ever heard." After I conversed with him for a few
minutes, he told me that he was dyslexic, and knew about
the pains of growing up with a learning disability. He never
told any of his friends before... Thank you for listening.

Signed: A. F.

Dear Mr. Keyes,

For all of my life, I've been a bright child—getting top
grades and joining the gifted program—but these things
I was blessed with, I took for granted. I never actually
stopped and thought about just how lucky I was, that is,
until I read your short story, "Flowers for Algernon."
"Flowers for Algernon" had a very big impact on my life,
and how I feel about the lives of others. It opened my eyes
to how cruel our society can be to a mentally challenged
person.

There is a man...who lives down my Grandma's road. Five days a week, he rides his bike to his brother's plant nursery to work and usually stops to talk to my Grandma when she's on her front porch. He is in his forties but has the mind of a child. Each time we see him, he smiles, waves, and joyously calls, "Hi-i-i Ruthie!" to my Grandma.

Once, [he] told my Grandma that, at the nursery, a 7-foot-tall tree fell on him when he was moving it. He said that the people around him just pointed and laughed even though he needed help. His story reminded me of Charlie's co-workers that made fun of him.

I think that your story is a very beneficial contribution to our literature today. It stimulates our minds by inducing creative thought about operations such as Charlie's and it pulls at our emotions through Charlie's accomplishments and failures. I think that if everyone were to read "Flowers for Algernon," we could make our society better suited for, and much kinder to, the mentally challenged.

Thank you so much for writing such a wonderful story to share with us. Keep writing.

Signed: S. B.

Dear Daniel Keyes,

I have recently re-read "Flowers for Algernon" and was surprised at how I'd forgotten how encouraging, support-ive, and educating your story was. Once again, I was truly inspired...

"Flowers for Algernon" is encouraging to me because it helps me to remember to be patient with those who are slower than I am. I am more willing to help others and lend support. Your character's purity and inner strength show the undeniable need for kindness and knowledge in the world today. Most important though, it educated me (and many others I am sure) to be thankful for what I am blessed with.

Signed: K. R.

I pointed to the students at the front table, and held up their letters to the audience. "When that boy said to me, 'Mr. Keyes, I want to be smart,' he gave me the voice and character of Charlie. I dropped it like a pebble into the ocean. And now, it still spreads ripples, into the hearts of young people, like these three, whose letters I shared with you tonight—letters that were a gift to me this morning."

The conference ended on that note, but I've thought about it since. In my childhood, my love of books led me to want to become a writer. In my early thirties, when I believed I was dying without the novel ever being published and thought I was looking into the abyss of my mortality, I'd said, "Thank God I finished the book." That's when I knew I was a writer.

Now, in my own senior years, when I read letters like these from my readers, I understand *why* I write, and *why* I'll keep writing as long as I can. I write in the hope that, long after I'm gone, my stories and books, like pebbles dropped into water, will continue to spread in widening circles and touch other minds. Possibly, other minds in conflict with themselves.

The second most frequently asked question is about the ending. Since Algernon dies, does that mean that Charlie also dies? Or did I intentionally leave it open-ended for a sequel?

As I've said earlier, I do not believe a writer should interpret or explain the meanings or intentions of a particular work, so I always answer, "I don't know."

Yet, over the years, I have always felt Charlie's presence. All I can say is, I still see him in that classroom, fifty years ago, walking up to my desk and stopping to say, "Mr. Keyes, I want to be smart."

Wherever he is, whatever he's doing, I will never forget those words that gave me the key to unlock the story and the novel. His words have touched tens of millions of readers and moviegoers around the world. And they've changed my life as well.

Because of him, I'm a lot smarter now than I was the day his path crossed mine.

AFTERWORD

||||||||||||||||||||||||||

MY "WHAT WOULD HAPPEN IF . . . ?" IS HAPPENING

I'VE DISCOVERED THAT ONE of the methods high school teachers and college professors use in discussing "Flowers for Algernon" is to stimulate debate about the morality of using science to increase animal or human intelligence if fiction ever became a reality. That issue hit home far sooner than I expected.

On the morning of September 2, 1999, after I'd finished what I believed was the final chapter of this book, I decided to celebrate with my favorite breakfast at a local restaurant. The waiter delivered my order, and I propped up the *New York Times* to read while I ate. When I saw the front-page headline, I dropped my fork.

SCIENTIST CREATES A SMARTER MOUSE
WORK ON FORMATION OF MEMORY
MAY SOMEDAY HELP PEOPLE

The idea that had crossed my mind on a train station more than fifty years earlier—"What would happen if it were possible to increase a person's intelligence?"—had found its way into the laboratories of Molecular Biology at Princeton, of Brain and

Cognitive Science at MIT, and of Anesthesiology and Neurobiology at Washington University in St. Louis.

The *Times* was reporting on an article called "Genetic enhancement of learning and memory in mice," published in that day's issue of the journal *Nature*. Dr. Joe Z. Tsien, a neurobiologist at Princeton, and his research team, described how they had altered genes in mice embryos and discovered a "graded switch for memory formation."

The gene *NR2B* is crucial to learning because it helps build the protein that acts as a receptor for specific chemical signals we experience as memories. This receptor is plentiful in young mice, but drops off drastically after sexual maturity. By adding more of this single gene to mouse embryos, they were able to make the embryos grow up as more intelligent mice.

Also, the offspring of these genetically altered mice, according to Dr. Tsien, "exhibit superior ability in learning and memory in various behavioral tasks." Scientists believe that adults whose memory and learning genes are boosted in this way might be able to develop the learning skills of youngsters.

The *smart mice* outperformed *wild mice* in several tests, such as the speed of remembering the location of a submerged platform hidden below murky water. Also, mice generally respond to familiar objects and new objects with equal interest. But in these tests the smart mice showed significantly greater interest in new objects—a sign of improved memory in recalling the familiar objects.

In two other experiments, gene-altered mice and their offspring displayed superior emotional memory as well. They were quicker to respond to a threat than the wild mice. After having been placed into a box and then given a mild shock, they were quicker at learning to fear the box itself, as evidenced by flinching, running, jumping, or squeaking.

But when the shock was discontinued, no longer associated with the box, the super-mice were quicker to learn not to fear the box. Conditioned behavior, and deconditioning behavior, both obviously survival traits, displayed what the scientists called emotional intelligence, what some contemporary neuropsychologists now call E.Q.

I stared at my uneaten cold breakfast, paid the bill, and went back to my office to finish reading the article. Then I checked out the Internet to see what the response had been to the new discoveries. Just as I had expected, controversy had surfaced quickly, among scientists as well as the media.

Dr. Eric R. Kandel, a leading brain expert at Columbia University, who praised the quality and reliability of Dr. Tsien's work, told the *New York Times* that the first applications of Dr. Tsien's work should be medical—helping those with memory loss. Kandel responded to the idea of enhancing *normal* intelligence as "*neurobiological cosmetics*... a very slippery turf from a moral point of view..." He was quoted as saying, "It's one thing to improve memory in people with a memory deficit. But to begin to mess around with normal memory is tricky. I don't think we want to emphasize in society that intelligence is the only factor that counts... I wouldn't want to come across with some simplistic view that 'Take this pill' and we could produce a superior race."

Dr. Stevens of the Salk Institute told the *Times,* "It may be that learning things too well is bad... We could be stuck learning things we don't want to learn and our hard disks would be full of too much information."

In a story, illustrated with a Frankenstein monster–like child, *Time* magazine quoted UCLA neurobiologist Alcino Silva, "Everything comes at a price... Very often when there's a genetic change where we improve, something else gets hit by it, so it's never a clean thing.

Jeremy Rifkin, identified only as "a long time biotech critic," is quoted: "How do you know you've not going to create a mental monster? . . . We may be on the road to programming our own extinction."

I finally phoned the lead researcher at Princeton, Dr. Joe Z. Tsien. I introduced myself, and told him I would like to mention his work briefly at the end of the new book I was writing. He said that would please him. After we discussed his experiments in general, I asked, "How do you respond to criticism about the moral implications of applying so-called genetic engineering to humans by enhancing intelligence?"

"The very definition of enhancement is actually based on what is healthy or normal," he said. "I am now thirty-six years old, and my memory is not as good as it was earlier. Is it part of getting older and dying, or is it a disease? Many things we accepted as part of aging are now known as diseases, and we can use therapeutic drugs for memory loss.

"I am not driven by the need to create a super-mouse or super-genius," he said, "but we have found the right gene—the magic switch for memory formation. An individual with an I.Q. of 120 might feel he's disabled when compared to someone with and I.Q. of 160 to 170."

"So, you do believe it will be possible to increase human intelligence."

"Yes, but the jump from mice to humans is a huge jump," he said. "We will make that jump. *It will happen.* It's time for us to discuss these issues."

Dr. Tsien had been quoted in the *Times* as believing that improving people's intelligence, whether by drugs or genetic alteration, could have profound effects throughout society. I asked him about that.

"Civilization is based on our extraordinary human intelligence," he said. "That is why our society evolves and civilization evolves. And if there is a way to enhance [human] intelligence then it may not be surprising to see a change in the evolution of society."

We spoke briefly of *Flowers for Algernon*.

"Of course, I read it," he said. "Everyone is talking about it. When I finished it, I said, 'Wow! Gosh! He's so far ahead of us, we'll never catch up!'"

Now that they'd caught up to Algernon, I couldn't help thinking about the Charlies of the world. I asked, "How long do you think it will take to increase *human* intelligence?"

"You writers are always ahead of us. We just follow you."

"How long?" I asked again.

After a long pause, Dr. Tsien said, "I expect it to happen in the next thirty years."

ACKNOWLEDGMENTS

MOST PEOPLE WHOSE LIVES crossed my writing life are described in this autobiography. I thank them here again.

However, since novelettes, novels, live teleplays, theatrical movies, amateur stage dramas, Broadway musicals, and TV movies do not provide an opportunity for the author to mention others, or to elaborate on his debt of gratitude, I wish now to acknowledge the following people.

The late Morton Klass, close friend, with whom I was able to share ideas and a chessboard on Hoffman Island, introduced me to science fiction, its writers, editors and the Hydra Club.

Through Mort, I met his brother, Philip Klass (pseudonym William Tenn) who gave generously of his time and judgment by reading my earliest stories. Phil was my first encounter with a tough, professional writer, who loved words, sentences, and paragraphs, and knew how to explain what he was criticizing or praising. When he read the first draft of the novelette version, he said, "Dan, this will become a classic." I am in his debt for his encouragement.

When the late Robert P. Mills, at the urging of Phil Klass, bought the original novelette version of "Flowers for Algernon" for *The Magazine of Fantasy and Science Fiction*, he set me on the path I walk today. Thanks, also, to Ed Ferman, of Mercury Press for publishing it.

I should like to express my appreciation to three attorneys: to Don Engel, in Los Angeles, who, after his success in winning the arbitration for the dramatic-musical rights in 1977, became my agent-attorney.

Engel later arranged for me to join the William Morris Agency in Beverly Hills, where I worked with Ron Nolte, who battled vigorously for my contract rights and proved that the William Morris Agency backs up its writers.

I can't find enough words of praise for Eric Zohn, brilliant young attorney in the Morris New York office. Eric was always there when I needed him to untangle the knottiest legal problems. Many thanks to my present literary agent Mel Berger, at the William Morris Agency, for his constant encouragement.

In Japan, I wish to thank Mr. Hiroshi Hayakawa of Hayakawa Publishing who brought *Flowers for Algernon* to Japan in 1978. One and a half million hardcover copies are in print in Japan.

Tatemi Sakai, agent with the Orion Literary Agency, negotiated theatrical productions of *Flowers for Algernon* and the Japanese contract for *The Fifth Sally*.

Miyo Kai, agent with the Tuttle-Mori Literary Agency in Japan, subagent of the Morris Agency, negotiated Japanese contracts for most of my other books with Hayakawa Shobo.

My new independent editor, Sol Stein, formerly of Stein and Day Publishers, encouraged me to develop and revise this autobiography. I thank him for his insights and advice.

Thanks to David Ginsberg, president of Citadel Entertainment, and to Craig Zadan and Neil Meron of Storyline Entertainment, for their confidence and their efforts in the long arbitration struggle to confirm my rights in the CBS-TV made-for-television movie production of *Flowers for Algernon*.

My debt to my parents goes far beyond the relationship described in these pages. My father provided the mountain of books and passed on to me the yearning to lift myself out of poverty through education. My mother taught me to seek perfection but also to care about other people. Both were tough taskmasters, but—though long gone—their influence has cast a long and loving shadow over my life and this book.

My thanks to other members of my family:

To my sister Gail, and my brother-in-law Ed Marcus, for their unstinting hospitality, and for their understanding that although we reside so close in the real world, in my mind—when I write—I live in other times and other places.

To my wife Aurea, always by my side as a sharp-eyed editor and critic; to my daughter and confidant, Leslie Joan, for never letting things grow dull, and for reading and making helpful suggestions on this book in manuscript; and to my daughter Hillary Ann, my personal assistant—herself a lover of books—who was an indispensable part of the hardcover from the first idea through the artwork and design, to the last revision. I thank these, my loved ones, who put up with me, encouraged me, and gave me the emotional support every working writer needs.

Finally, Charlie Gordon and Algernon would never have existed if not for the developmentally challenged boy whose yearning for intelligence made him come up to me in the classroom, and say: "Mr. Keyes, I want to be smart." Although he remains anonymous, and cannot know the effect of those words, I and my readers owe him more than we can say.

DANIEL KEYES
OCTOBER 31, 1999

Flowers for Algernon

THE ORIGINAL NOVELETTE

progris riport 1—martch 5

Dr. Strauss says I shud rite down what I think and evrey thing that happins to me from now on. I dont know why but he says its importint so they will see if they will use me. I hope they use me. Miss Kinnian says maybe they can make me smart. I want to be smart. My name is Charlie Gordon. I am 37 years old and 2 weeks ago was my brithday. I have nuthing more to rite now so I will close for today.

progris riport 2—martch 6

I had a test today. I think I faled it. and I think that mabye now they wont use me. What happind is a nice young man was in the room and he had some white cards with ink spillled all over them. He sed Charlie what do you see on this card. I was very skared even tho I had my rabits foot in my pockit because when I was a kid I always faled tests in school and I spillled ink to. I told him I saw a inkblot. He said yes and it made me feel good. I thot that was all but when I got up to go he stopped me. He said now sit down Charlie we are not thru yet. Then I dont

remember so good but he wantid me to say what was in the ink.
I dint see nuthing in the ink but he said there was picturs there
other pepul saw some picturs. I coudnt see any picturs. I reely
tryed to see. I held the card close up and then far away. Then I
said if I had my glases I coud see better I usally only ware my
glases in the movies or TV but I said they are in the closit in the
hall. I got them. Then I said let me see that card agen I bet Ill
find it now.

I tryed hard but I still coudnt find the picturs I only saw the
ink. I told him maybe I need new glases. He rote somthing
down on a paper and I got skared of faling the test. I told him it
was a very nice inkblot with littel points all around the eges. He
looked very sad so that wasnt it. I said please let me try agen. Ill
get it in a few minits becaus Im not so fast somtimes. Im a slow
reeder too in Miss Kinnians class for slow adults but I'm trying
very hard.

He gave me a chance with another card that had 2 kinds of
ink spillled on it red and blue.

He was very nice and talked slow like Miss Kinnian does and
he explaned it to me that it was a raw shok. He said pepul see
things in the ink. I said show me where. He said think. I told
him I think a inkblot but that wasnt rite eather. He said what
does it remind you-pretend something. I closd my eyes for a
long time to pretend. I told him I pretned a fowntan pen with
ink leeking all over a table cloth. Then he got up and went out.

I dont think I passd the *raw shok* test.

progris report 3—martch 7

Dr Strauss and Dr Nemur say it dont matter about the inkblots.
I told them I dint spill the ink on the cards and I coudnt see anything in the ink. They said that maybe they will still use me. I
said Miss Kinnian never gave me tests like that one only spelling

and reading. They said Miss Kinnian told that I was her bestist pupil in the adult nite scool becaus I tryed the hardist and I reely wantid to lern. They said how come you went to the adult nite scool all by yourself Charlie. How did you find it. I said I askd pepul and sum-body told me where I shud go to lern to read and spell good. They said why did you want to. I told them becaus all my life I wantid to he smart and not dumb. But its very hard to be smart. They said you know it will probly be tempirery. I said yes Miss Kinnian told me. I dont care if it herts.

Later I had more crazy tests today. The nice lady who gave it me told me the name and I asked her how do you spellit so I can rite it in my progris riport. THEMATIC APPERCEPTION TEST. I dont know the frist 2 words but I know what test means. You got to pass it or you get bad marks. This test lookd easy becaus I coud see the picturs. Only this time she dint want me to tell her the picturs. That mixd me up. I said the man yesterday said I shoud tell him what I saw in the ink she said that dont make no difrence. She said make up storys about the pepul in the picturs.

I told her how can you tell storys about pepul you never met. I said why shud I make up lies. I never tell lies any more becaus I always get caut.

She told me this test and the other one the raw-shok was for getting personalty. I laffed so hard. I said how can you get that thing from inkblots and fotos. She got sore and put her picturs away. I dont care. It was sily. I gess I faled that test too.

Later some men in white coats took me to a difernt part of the hospitil and gave me a game to play. It was like a race with a white mouse. They called the mouse Algernon. Algernon was in a box with a lot of twists and turns like all kinds of walls and they gave me a pencil and a paper with lines and lots of boxes. On one side it said START and on the other end it said FINISH. They said it

was amazed and that Algernon and me had the same amazed to
do. I dint see how we could have the same amazed if Algernon
had a box and I had a paper but I dint say nothing. Anyway there
wasnt time because the race started.

One of the men had a watch he was trying to hide so I
woudnt see it so I tryed not to look and that made me nervus.
Anyway that test made me feel worser than all the others because
they did it over 10 times with difernt amazeds and Algernon
won every time. I dint know that mice were so smart. Maybe
thats because Algernon is a white mouse. Maybe white mice are
smarter then other mice.

progris riport 4—Mar 8

Their going to use me! Im so exited I can hardly write. Dr
Nemur and Dr Strauss had a argament about it first. Dr Nemur
was in the office when Dr Strauss brot me in. Dr Nemur was
worryed about using me but Dr Strauss told him Miss Kinnian
rekemmended me the best from all the people who she was
teaching. I like Miss Kinnian becaus shes a very smart teacher.
And she said Charlie your going to have a second chance. If you
volenteer for this experament you mite get smart. They dont
know if it will be perminint but theirs a chance. Thats why I said
ok even when I was scared because she said it was an operashun.
She said dont be scared Charlie you done so much with so little
I think you deserv it most of all.

So I got scaird when Dr Nemur and Dr Strauss argud about
it. Dr Strauss said I had something that was very good. He said
I had a good *motor-vation*. I never even knew I had that. I felt
proud when he said that not every body with an eye-q of 68 had
that thing. I dont know what it is or where I got it but he said
Algernon had it too. Algernons *motor-vation* is the cheese they
put in his box. But it cant be that because I didnt eat any cheese
this week.

Then he told Dr Nemur something I dint understand so while they were talking I wrote down some of the words.

He said Dr Nemur I know Charlie is not what you had in mind as the first of your new brede of intelek** (coudnt get the word) superman. But most people of his low ment** are host** and uncoop** they are usualy dull apath** and hard to reach. He has a good natcher hes intristed and eager to please.

Dr Nemur said remember he will be the first human beeng ever to have his intelijence trippled by surgicle meens.

Dr Strauss said exakly. Look at how well hes lerned to read and write for his low mentel age its as grate an acheve** as you and I lerning einstines therey of **vity without help. That shows the intenss motor-vation. Its comparat** a tremen** achev ** I say we use Charlie.

I dint get all the words and they were talking to fast but it sounded like Dr Strauss was on my side and like the other one wasnt.

Then Dr Nemur nodded he said all right maybe your right. We will use Charlie. When he said that I got so exited I jumped up and shook his hand for being so good to me. I told him thank you doc you wont be sorry for giving me a second chance. And I mean it like I told him. After the operashun Im gonna try to be smart. Im gonna try awful hard.

progris ript 5—Mar 10

Im skared. Lots of people who work here and the nurses and the people who gave me the tests came to bring me candy and wish me luck. I hope I have luck. I got my rabits foot and my lucky penny and my horse shoe. Only a black cat crossed me when I was comming to the hospitil. Dr Strauss says dont be supersitis Charlie this is sience. Anyway Im keeping my rabits foot with me.

I asked Dr Strauss if Ill beat Algernon in the race after the operashun and he said maybe. If the operashun works Ill show that mouse I can be as smart as he is. Maybe smarter. Then Ill be abel to read better and spell the words good and know lots of things and be like other people. I want to be smart like other people. If it works perminint they will make everybody smart all over the wurld.

They dint give me anything to eat this morning. I dont know what that eating has to do with getting smart. Im very hungry and Dr Nemur took away my box of candy. That Dr Nemur is a grouch. Dr Strauss says I can have it back after the operashun. You cant eat befor a operashun.

Progress Report 6—Mar 15

The operashun dint hurt. He did it while I was sleeping. They took off the bandijis from my eyes and my head today so I can make a PROGRESS REPORT. Dr Nemur who looked at some of my other ones says I spell PROGRESS wrong and he told me how to spell it and REPORT too. I got to try and remember that.

I have a very bad memary for spelling. Dr Strauss says its Ok to tell about all the things that happin to me but he says I shoud tell more about what I feel and what I think. When I told him I dont know how to think he said try. All the time when the bandijis were on my eyes I tryed to think. Nothing happened. I dont know what to think about. Maybe if I ask him he will tell me how I can think now that Im suppose to get smart. What do smart people think about. Fancy things I suppose. I wish I knew some fancy things alredy.

Progress Report 7—Mar 19

Nothing is happining. I had lots of tests and different kinds of races with Algernon. I hate that mouse. He always beats me. Dr Strauss said I got to play those games. And he said some time I got to take those tests over again. These inkblots are stupid. And those pictures are stupid too. I like to draw a picture of a man and a woman but I wont make up lies about people.

I got a headache from trying to think so much. I thot Dr Strauss was my frend but he dont help me. He dont tell me what to think or when Ill get smart. Miss Kinnian dint come to see me. I think writing these progress reports are stupid too.

Progress Report 8—Mar 23

Im going back to work at the factery. They said it was better I shud go back to work but I cant tell anyone what the operashun was for and I have to come to the hospitil for an hour evry night after work. They are gonna pay me mony every month for lerning to be smart. Im glad Im going back to work because I miss my job and all my frends and all the fun we have there.

Dr Strauss says I shud keep writing things down but I dont have to do it every day just when I think of something or something speshul happins. He says dont get discoridged because it takes time and it happins slow. He says it took a long time with Algernon before he got 3 times smarter then he was before. Thats why Algernon beats me all the time because he had that operashun too. That makes me feel better. I coud probly do that *amazed* faster than a reglar mouse. Maybe some day Ill beat Algernon. Boy that would be something. So far Algernon looks like he mite be smart perminent.

Mar 25 (I dont have to write PROGRESS REPORT on top any more just when I hand it in once a week for Dr Nemur to read. I just have to put the date on. That saves time)

We had a lot of fun at the factery today. Joe Carp said hey look where Charlie had his operashun what did they do Charlie put some brains in. I was going to tell him but I remembered Dr Strauss said no. Then Frank Reilly said what did you do Charlie forget your key and open your door the hard way. That made me laff. Their really my friends and they like me.

Sometimes somebody will say hey look at Joe or Frank or George he really pulled a Charlie Gordon. I dont know why they say that but they always laff. This morning Amos Borg who is the 4 man at Donnegans used my name when he shouted at Ernie the office boy. Ernie lost a packige. He said Ernie for god-sake what are you trying to be a Charlie Gordon. I dont understand why he said that. I never lost any packiges.

Mar 28 Dr Strauss came to my room tonight to see why I dint come in like I was suppose to. I told him I dont like to race with Algernon any more. He said I dont have to for a while but I shud come in. He had a present for me only it wasnt a present but just for lend. I thot it was a little television but it wasnt. He said I got to turn it on when I go to sleep. I said your kidding why shud I turn it on when Im going to sleep. Who ever herd of a thing like that. But he said if I want to get smart I got to do what he says. I told him I dint think I was going to get smart and he put his hand on my sholder and said Charlie you dont know it yet but your getting smarter all the time. You wont notice for a while. I think he was just being nice to make me feel good because I dont look any smarter.

Oh yes I almost forgot. I asked him when I can go back to the class at Miss Kinnians school. He said I wont go their. He said that soon Miss Kinnian will come to the hospitil to start and teach me speshul. I was mad at her for not comming to see me when I got the operashun but I like her so maybe we will be frends again.

Mar 29 That crazy TV kept me up all night. How can I sleep with something yelling crazy things all night in my ears. And the nutty pictures. Wow. I dont know what it says when Im up so how am I going to know when Im sleeping.

Dr Strauss says its ok. He says my brains are lerning when I sleep and that will help me when Miss Kinnian starts my lessons in the hospitl (only I found out it isnt a hospitil its a labatory). I think its all crazy. If you can get smart when your sleeping why do people go to school. That thing I dont think will work. I use to watch the late show and the late late show on TV all the time and it never made me smart. Maybe you have to sleep while you watch it.

PROGRESS REPORT 9—April 3

Dr Strauss showed me how to keep the TV turned low so now I can sleep. I dont hear a thing. And I still dont understand what it says. A few times I play it over in the morning to find out what I lerned when I was sleeping and I dont think so. Miss Kinnian says Maybe its another langwidge or something. But most times it sounds american. It talks so fast faster then even Miss Gold who was my teacher in 6 grade and I remember she talked so fast I coudnt understand her.

I told Dr Strauss what good is it to get smart in my sleep. I want to be smart when Im awake. He says its the same thing and I have two minds. Theres the *subconscious* and the *conscious* (thats how you spell it). And one dont tell the other one what its doing. They dont even talk to each other. Thats why I dream. And boy have I been having crazy dreams. Wow. Ever since that night TV. The late late late late late show.

I forgot to ask him if it was only me or if everybody had those two minds.

(I just looked up the word in the dictionary Dr Strauss gave me. The word is *subconscious. adj. Of the nature of mental opera-tions yet not present in consciousness; as, subconscious conflict of desires.*) Theres more but I still don't know what it means. This isnt a very good dictionary for dumb people like me. Anyway the headache is from the party. My frends from the factery Joe Carp and Frank Reilly invited me to go with them to Muggsys Saloon for some drinks. I dont like to drink but they said we will have lots of fun. I had a good time.

Joe Carp said I shoud show the girls how I mop out the toilet in the factory and he got me a mop. I showed them and everyone laffed when I told that Mr Donnegan said I was the best janiter he ever had because I like my job and do it good and never come late or miss a day except for my operashun.

I said Miss Kinnian always said Charlie be proud of your job because you do it good.

Everybody laffed and we had a good time and they gave me lots of drinks and Joe said Charlie is a card when hes potted. I dont know what that means but everybody likes me and we have fun. I cant wait to be smart like my best frends Joe Carp and Frank Reilly.

I dont remember how the party was over but I think I went out to buy a newspaper and coffe for Joe and Frank and when I came back there was no one their. I looked for them all over till late. Then I dont remember so good but I think I got sleepy or sick. A nice cop brot me back home. Thats what my landlady Mrs Flynn says.

But I got a headache and a big lump on my head and black and blue all over. I think maybe I fell but Joe Carp says it was the cop they beat up drunks some times. I don't think so. Miss Kinnian says cops are to help people. Anyway I got a bad headache and Im sick and hurt all over. I dont think Ill drink anymore.

April 6 I beat Algernon! I dint even know I beat him until Burt the tester told me. Then the second time I lost because I got so exited I fell off the chair before I finished. But after that I beat him 8 more times. I must be getting smart to beat a smart mouse like Algernon. But I dont feel smarter.

I wanted to race Algernon some more but Burt said thats enough for one day. They let me hold him for a minit. Hes not so bad. Hes soft like a ball of cotton. He blinks and when he opens his eyes their black and pink on the eges.

I said can I feed him because I felt bad to beat him and I wanted to be nice and make frends. Burt said no Algernon is a very specshul mouse with an operashun like mine, and he was the first of all the animals to stay smart so long. He told me Algernon is so smart that every day he has to solve a test to get his food. Its a thing like a lock on a door that changes every time Algernon goes in to eat so he has to lern something new to get his food. That made me sad because if he coudnt lern he woud be hungry.

I dont think its right to make you pass a test to eat. How woud Dr Nemur like it to have to pass a test every time he wants to eat. I think Ill be frends with Algernon.

April 9   Tonight after work Miss Kinnian was at the laboratory. She looked like she was glad to see me but scared. I told her dont worry Miss Kinnian Im not smart yet and she laffed. She said I have confidence in you Charlie the way you struggled so hard to read and right better than all the others. At werst you will have it for a littel wile and your doing somthing for sience.

We are reading a very hard book. I never read such a hard book before. Its called *Robinson Crusoe* about a man who gets merooned on a dessert Iland. Hes smart and figers out all kinds of things so he can have a house and food and hes a good swimmer. Only I feel sorry because hes all alone and has no frends. But I think their must be somebody else on the iland because theres a picture with his funny umbrella looking at footprints. I hope he gets a frend and not be lonly.

April 10   Miss Kinnian teaches me to spell better. She says look at a word and close your eyes and say it over and over until you remember. I have lots of truble with *through* that you say *threw* and *enough* and *tough* that you dont say *enew* and *tew*. You got to say *enuff* and *tuff*. Thats how I use to write it before I started to get smart. Im confused but Miss Kinnian says theres no reason in spelling.

Apr 14   Finished *Robinson Crusoe*. I want to find out more about what happens to him but Miss Kinnian says thats all there is. *Why*

Apr 15   Miss Kinnian says Im lerning fast. She read some of the Progress Reports and she looked at me kind of funny. She says Im a fine person and Ill show them all. I asked her why. She said never mind but I shoudnt feel bad if I find out that everybody isnt nice like I think. She said for a person who god gave so little to you done more then a lot of people with brains they never even used. I said all my frends are smart people but there good. They like me and they never did anything that wasnt nice. Then she got something in her eye and she had to run out to the ladys room.

Apr 16   Today, I lerned, the *comma,* this is a comma (,) a period, with a tail, Miss Kinnian, says its importent, because, it makes writing, better, she said, somebody, coud lose, a lot of money, if a comma, isnt, in the, right place, I dont have, any money, and I dont see, how a comma, keeps you, from losing it,

   But she says, everybody, uses commas, so Ill use, them too,

Apr 17   I used the comma wrong. Its punctuation. Miss Kinnian told me to look up long words in the dictionary to lern to spell them. I said whats the difference if you can read it anyway. She said its part of your education so now on Ill look up all the words Im not sure how to spell. It takes a long time to write that way but I think Im remembering. I only have to look up once and after that I get it right. Anyway thats how come I got the word *punctuation* right. (Its that way in the dictionary). Miss Kinnian says a period is punctuation too, and there are lots of other marks to lern. I told her I thot all the periods had to have tails but she said no.

You got to mix them up, she showed? me" how. to mix! them(up,. and now; I can! mix up all kinds" of punctuation, in! my writing? There, are lots! of rules? to lern; but Im gettin'g them in my head.

One thing I? like about, Dear Miss Kinnian: (thats the way it goes in a business letter if I ever go into business) is she, always gives me' a reason" when—I ask. She's a gen'ius! I wish! I cou'd be smart" like, her;

(Punctuation, is; fun!)

April 18   What a dope I am! I didn't even understand what she was talking about. I read the grammar book last night and it explanes the whole thing. Then I saw it was the same way as Miss Kinnian was trying to tell me, but I didn't get it. I got up in the middle of the night, and the whole thing straightened out in my mind.

Miss Kinnian said that the TV working in my sleep helped out. She said I reached a plateau. Thats like the flat top of a hill.

After I figgered out how punctuation worked, I read over all my old Progress Reports from the beginning. Boy, did I have crazy spelling and punctuation! I told Miss Kinnian I ought to go over the pages and fix all the mistakes but she said, "No, Charlie, Dr. Nemur wants them just as they are. That's why he let you keep them after they were photostated, to see your own progress. You're coming along fast, Charlie."

That made me feel good. After the lesson I went down and played with Algernon. We don't race any more.

April 20   I feel sick inside. Not sick like for a doctor, but inside my chest it feels empty like getting punched and a heartburn at the same time.

I wasn't going to write about it, but I guess I got to, because it's important. Today was the first time I ever stayed home from work.

Last night Joe Carp and Frank Reilly invited me to a party. There were lots of girls and some men from the factory. I remembered how sick I got last time I drank too much, so I told Joe I didn't want anything to drink. He gave me a plain Coke instead. It tasted funny, but I thought it was just a bad taste in my mouth.

We had a lot of fun for a while. Joe said I should dance with Ellen and she would teach me the steps. I fell a few times and I couldn't understand why because no one else was dancing besides Ellen and me. And all the time I was tripping because somebody's foot was always sticking out.

Then when I got up I saw the look on Joe's face and it gave me a funny feeling in my stomack. "He's a scream," one of the girls said. Everybody was laughing.

Frank said, "I ain't laughed so much since we sent him off for the newspaper that night at Muggsy's and ditched him."

"Look at him. His face is red."

"He's blushing. Charlie is blushing."

"Hey, Ellen, what'd you do to Charlie? I never saw him act like that before."

I didn't know what to do or where to turn. Everyone was looking at me and laughing and I felt naked. I wanted to hide myself. I ran out into the street and I threw up. Then I walked home. It's a funny thing I never knew that Joe and Frank and the others liked to have me around all the time to make fun of me.

Now I know what it means when they say "to pull a Charlie Gordon."

I'm ashamed.

PROGRESS REPORT 11

April 21   Still didn't go into the factory. I told Mrs. Flynn my landlady to call and tell Mr. Donnegan I was sick. Mrs. Flynn looks at me very funny lately like she's scared of me.

I think it's a good thing about finding out how everybody laughs at me. I thought about it a lot. It's because I'm so dumb and I don't even know when I'm doing something dumb. People think it's funny when a dumb person can't do things the same way they can.

Anyway, now I know I'm getting smarter every day. I know punctuation and I can spell good. I like to look up all the hard words in the dictionary and I remember them. I'm reading a lot now, and Miss Kinnian says I read very fast. Sometimes I even understand what I'm reading about, and it stays in my mind. There are times when I can close my eyes and think of a page and it all comes back like a picture.

Besides history, geography, and arithmetic, Miss Kinnian said I should start to learn a few foreign languages. Dr. Strauss gave me some more tapes to play while I sleep. I still don't understand how that conscious and unconscious mind works, but Dr. Strauss says not to worry yet. He asked me to promise that when I start learning college subjects next week I wouldn't read any books on psychology—that is, until he gives me permission.

I feel a lot better today, but I guess I'm still a little angry that all the time people were laughing and making fun of me because I wasn't so smart. When I become intelligent like Dr. Strauss says, with three times my I.Q. of 68, then maybe I'll be like everyone else and people will like me and be friendly.

I'm not sure what an I.Q. is. Dr. Nemur said it was something that measured how intelligent you were—like a scale in the drugstore weighs pounds. But Dr. Strauss had a big argument with him and said an I.Q. didn't weigh intelligence at all. He said an I.Q. showed how much intelligence you could get, like the numbers on the outside of a measuring cup. You still had to fill the cup up with stuff.

Then when I asked Burt, who gives me my intelligence tests and works with Algernon, he said that both of them were wrong (only I had to promise not to tell them he said so). Burt says that the I.Q. measures a lot of different things including some of the things you learned already, and it really isn't any good at all.

So I still don't know what I.Q. is except that mine is going to be over 200 soon. I didn't want to say anything, but I don't see how if they don't know what it is, or where it is—I don't see how they know how much of it you've got.

Dr. Nemur says I have to take a Rorschach Test tomorrow. I wonder what that is.

April 22 I found out what a *Rorschach* is. It's the test I took before the operation—the one with the inkblots on the pieces of cardboard. The man who gave me the test was the same one.

I was scared to death of those inkblots. I knew he was going to ask me to find the pictures and I knew I wouldn't be able to. I was thinking to myself, if only there was some way of knowing what kind of pictures were hidden there. Maybe there weren't any pictures at all. Maybe it was just a trick to see if I was dumb enough to look for something that wasn't there. Just thinking about that made me sore at him.

"All right, Charlie," he said, "you've seen these cards before, remember?"

"Of course I remember."

The way I said it, he knew I was angry, and he looked surprised. "Yes, of course. Now I want you to look at this one. What might this be? What do you see on this card? People see all sorts of things in these inkblots. Tell me what it might be for you— what it makes you think of."

I was shocked. That wasn't what I had expected him to say at all. "You mean there are no pictures hidden in those inkblots?"

He frowned and took off his glasses. "What?"

"Pictures. Hidden in the inkblots. Last time you told me that everyone could see them and you wanted me to find them too."

He explained to me that the last time he had used almost the exact same words he was using now. I didn't believe it, and I still have the suspicion that he misled me at the time just for the fun of it. Unless—I don't know any more—could I have been that feebleminded?

We went through the cards slowly. One of them looked like a pair of bats tugging at something. Another one looked like two men fencing with swords. I imagined all sorts of things. I guess I got carried away. But I didn't trust him any more, and I kept turning them around and even looking on the back to see if there was anything there I was supposed to catch. While he was making his notes, I peeked out of the corner of my eye to read it. But it was all in code that looked like this:

WF+A DdF-Ad orig. WF-A SF+obj

The test still doesn't make sense to me. It seems to me that anyone could make up lies about things that they didn't really see. How could he know I wasn't making a fool of him by mentioning things that I didn't really imagine? Maybe I'll understand it when Dr. Strauss lets me read up on psychology.

April 25 I figured out a new way to line up the machines in the factory, and Mr. Donnegan says it will save him ten thousand dollars a year in labor and increased production. He gave me a twenty-five-dollar bonus.

I wanted to take Joe Carp and Frank Reilly out to lunch to celebrate, but Joe said he had to buy some things for his wife, and Frank said he was meeting his cousin for lunch. I guess it'll take a little time for them to get used to the changes in me. Everybody seems to be frightened of me. When I went over to Amos Borg and tapped him on the shoulder, he jumped up in the air.

People don't talk to me much any more or kid around the way they used to. It makes the job kind of lonely.

April 27 I got up the nerve today to ask Miss Kinnian to have dinner with me tomorrow night to celebrate my bonus.

At first she wasn't sure it was right, but I asked Dr. Strauss and he said it was okay. Dr. Strauss and Dr. Nemur don't seem to be getting along so well. They're arguing all the time. This evening when I came in to ask Dr. Strauss about having dinner with Miss Kinnian, I heard them shouting. Dr. Nemur was saying that it was his experiment and his research, and Dr. Strauss was shouting back that he contributed just as much, because he found me through Miss Kinnian and he performed the operation. Dr. Strauss said that someday thousands of neurosurgeons might be using his technique all over the world.

Dr. Nemur wanted to publish the results of the experiment at the end of this month. Dr. Strauss wanted to wait a while longer to be sure. Dr. Strauss said that Dr. Nemur was more interested in the Chair of Psychology at Princeton than he was in the experiment. Dr. Nemur said that Dr. Strauss was nothing but an opportunist who was trying to ride to glory on his coattails.

When I left afterwards, I found myself trembling. I don't know why for sure, but it was as if I'd seen both men clearly for the first time. I remember hearing Burt say that Dr. Nemur had a shrew of a wife who was pushing him all the time to get things published so that he could become famous. Burt said that the dream of her life was to have a big-shot husband.

Was Dr. Strauss really trying to ride on his coattails?

April 28 I don't understand why I never noticed how beautiful Miss Kinnian really is. She has brown eyes and feathery brown hair that comes to the top of her neck. She's only thirty-four! I think from the beginning I had the feeling that she was an unreachable genius—and very, very old. Now, every time I see her she grows younger and more lovely.

We had dinner and a long talk. When she said that I was coming along so fast that soon I'd be leaving her behind, I laughed.

"It's true, Charlie. You're already a better reader than I am. You can read a whole page at a glance while I can take in only a few lines at a time. And you remember every single thing you read. I'm lucky if I can recall the main thoughts and the general meaning."

"I don't feel intelligent. There are so many things I don't understand."

She took out a cigarette and I lit it for her. "You've got to be a *little* patient. You're accomplishing in days and weeks what it takes normal people to do in half a lifetime. That's what makes it so amazing. You're like a giant sponge now, soaking things in. Facts, figures, general knowledge. And soon you'll begin to connect them, too. You'll see how the different branches of learning are related. There are many levels, Charlie, like steps on a giant ladder that take you up higher and higher to see more and more of the world around you.

"I can see only a little bit of that, Charlie, and I won't go much higher than I am now, but you'll keep climbing up and up, and see more and more, and each step will open new worlds that you never even knew existed." She frowned. "I hope... I just hope to God—"

"What?"

"Never mind, Charles. I just hope I wasn't wrong to advise you to go into this in the first place."

I laughed. "How could that be? It worked, didn't it? Even Algernon is still smart."

We sat there silently for a while and I knew what she was thinking about as she watched me toying with the chain of my rabbit's foot and my keys. I didn't want to think of that possibility any more than elderly people want to think of death. I *knew* that this was only the beginning. I knew what she meant about levels because I'd seen some of them already. The thought of leaving her behind made me sad.

I'm in love with Miss Kinnian.

PROGRESS REPORT 12

April 30 I've quit my job with Donnegan's Plastic Box Company. Mr. Donnegan insisted that it would be better for all concerned if I left. What did I do to make them hate me so?

The first I knew of it was when Mr. Donnegan showed me the petition. Eight hundred and forty names, everyone connected with the factory except Fanny Girden. Scanning the list quickly, I saw at once that hers was the only missing name. All the rest demanded that I be fired.

Joe Carp and Frank Reilly wouldn't talk to me about it. No

one else would either, except Fanny. She was one of the few people I'd known who set her mind to something and believed it no matter what the rest of the world proved, said, or did—and Fanny did not believe that I should have been fired. She had been against the petition on principle and despite the pressure and threats she'd held out.

"Which don't mean to say," she remarked, "that I don't think there's something mighty strange about you, Charlie. Them changes. I don't know. You used to be a good, dependable, ordinary man—not too bright maybe, but honest. Who knows what you done to yourself to get so smart all of a sudden. Like everybody around here's been saying, Charlie, it's not right."

"But how can you say that, Fanny? What's wrong with a man becoming intelligent and wanting to acquire knowledge and understanding of the world around him?"

She stared down at her work and I turned to leave. Without looking at me, she said: "It was evil when Eve listened to the snake and ate from the tree of knowledge. It was evil when she saw that she was naked. If not for that none of us would ever have to grow old and sick, and die."

Once again now I have the feeling of shame burning inside me. This intelligence has driven a wedge between me and all the people I once knew and loved. Before, they laughed at me and despised me for my ignorance and dullness; now, they hate me for my knowledge and understanding. What in God's name do they want of me?

They've driven me out of the factory. Now I'm more alone than ever before...

May 15   Dr. Strauss is very angry at me for not having written any progress reports in two weeks. He's justified because the lab is now paying me a regular salary. I told him I was too busy thinking and reading. When I pointed out that writing was such a slow process that it made me impatient with my poor handwriting, he suggested that I learn to type. It's much easier to write now because I can type nearly seventy-five words a minute. Dr. Strauss continually reminds me of the need to speak and write simply so that people will be able to understand me.

I'll try to review all the things that happened to me during the last two weeks. Algernon and I were presented to the American Psychological Association sitting in convention with the World Psychological Association last Tuesday. We created quite a sensation. Dr. Nemur and Dr. Strauss were proud of us.

I suspect that Dr. Nemur, who is sixty—ten years older than Dr. Strauss—finds it necessary to see tangible results of his work. Undoubtedly the result of pressure by Mrs. Nemur.

Contrary to my earlier impressions of him, I realize that Dr. Nemur is not at all a genius. He has a very good mind, but it struggles under the spectre of self-doubt. He wants people to take him for a genius. Therefore, it is important for him to feel that his work is accepted by the world. I believe that Dr. Nemur was afraid of further delay because he worried that someone else might make a discovery along these lines and take the credit from him.

Dr. Strauss on the other hand might be called a genius, although I feel that his areas of knowledge are too limited. He was educated in the tradition of narrow specialization; the broader aspects of background were neglected far more than necessary— even for a neurosurgeon.

I was shocked to learn that the only ancient languages he could read were Latin, Greek, and Hebrew, and that he knows almost nothing of mathematics beyond the elementary levels of the calculus of variations. When he admitted this to me, I found myself almost annoyed. It was as if he'd hidden this part of himself in order to deceive me, pretending—as do many people I've discovered—to be what he is not. No one I've ever known is what he appears to be on the surface.

Dr. Nemur appears to be uncomfortable around me. Sometimes when I try to talk to him, he just looks at me strangely and turns away. I was angry at first when Dr. Strauss told me I was giving Dr. Nemur an inferiority complex. I thought he was mocking me and I'm oversensitive at being made fun of.

How was I to know that a highly respected psychoexperimentalist like Nemur was unacquainted with Hindustani and Chinese? It's absurd when you consider the work that is being done in India and China today in the very field of his study.

I asked Dr. Strauss how Nemur could refute Rahajamati's attack on his method and results if Nemur couldn't even read them in the first place. That strange look on Dr. Strauss' face can mean only one of two things. Either he doesn't want to tell Nemur what they're saying in India, or else—and this worries me—Dr. Strauss doesn't know either. I must be careful to speak and write clearly and simply so that people won't laugh.

May 18   I am very disturbed. I saw Miss Kinnian last night for the first time in over a week. I tried to avoid all discussions of intellectual concepts and to keep the conversation on a simple, everyday level, but she just stared at me blankly and asked me what I meant about the mathematical variance equivalent in Dorbermann's *Fifth Concerto*.

When I tried to explain she stopped me and laughed. I guess I got angry, but I suspect I'm approaching her on the wrong level. No matter what I try to discuss with her, I am unable to communicate. I must review Vrostadt's equations on *Levels of Semantic Progression*. I find that I don't communicate with people much any more. Thank God for books and music and things I can think about. I am alone in my apartment at Mrs. Flynn's boardinghouse most of the time and seldom speak to anyone.

May 20   I would not have noticed the new dishwasher, a boy of about sixteen, at the corner diner where I take my evening meals if not for the incident of the broken dishes. They crashed to the floor, shattering and sending bits of white china under the tables. The boy stood there, dazed and frightened, holding the empty tray in his hand. The whistles and catcalls from the customers (the cries of "hey, there go the profits!"... *"Mazeltov!"*... and "well, he didn't work here very long..." which invariably seems to follow the breaking of glass or dishware in a public restaurant) all seemed to confuse him.

When the owner came to see what the excitement was about, the boy cowered as if he expected to be struck and threw up his arms as if to ward off the blow.

"All right! All right, you dope," shouted the owner, "don't just stand there! Get the broom and sweep that mess up. A broom... a broom, you idiot! It's in the kitchen. Sweep up all the pieces."

The boy saw that he was not going to be punished. His frightened expression disappeared and he smiled and hummed as he came back with the broom to sweep the floor. A few of the rowdier customers kept up the remarks, amusing themselves at his expense.

"Here, sonny, there's a nice piece behind you..."

"C'mon, do it again..."

"He's not so dumb. It's easier to break 'em than to wash 'em..."

As his vacant eyes moved across the crowd of amused onlookers, he slowly mirrored their smiles and finally broke into an uncertain grin at the joke which he obviously did not understand.

I felt sick inside as I looked at his dull, vacuous smile, the wide, bright eyes of a child, uncertain but eager to please. They were laughing at him because he was mentally retarded.

And I had been laughing at him too.

Suddenly, I was furious at myself and all those who were smirking at him. I jumped up and shouted, "Shut up! Leave him alone! It's not his fault he can't understand! He can't help what he is! But for God's sake...he's still a human being!"

The room grew silent. I cursed myself for losing control and creating a scene. I tried not to look at the boy as I paid my check and walked out without touching my food. I felt ashamed for both of us.

How strange it is that people of honest feelings and sensibility, who would not take advantage of a man born without arms or legs or eyes—how such people think nothing of abusing a man born with low intelligence. It infuriated me to think that not too long ago I, like this boy, had foolishly played the clown.

And I had almost forgotten.

I'd hidden the picture of the old Charlie Gordon from myself because now that I was intelligent it was something that had to be pushed out of my mind. But today in looking at that boy, for the first time I saw what I had been. *I was just like him!*

Only a short time ago, I learned that people laughed at me. Now I can see that unknowingly I joined with them in laughing at myself. That hurts most of all.

I have often reread my progress reports and seen the illiteracy, the childish naïveté, the mind of low intelligence peering from a dark room, through the keyhole, at the dazzling light outside. I see that even in my dullness I knew that I was inferior, and that other people had something I lacked—something denied me. In my mental blindness, I thought that it was somehow connected with the ability to read and write, and I was sure that if I could get those skills I would automatically have intelligence too. Even a feeble-minded man wants to be like other men. A child may not know how to feed itself, or what to eat, yet it knows of hunger.

This then is what I was like, I never knew. Even with my gift of intellectual awareness, I never really knew.

This day was good for me. Seeing the past more clearly, I have decided to use my knowledge and skills to work in the field of increasing human intelligence levels. Who is better equipped for this work? Who else has lived in both worlds? These are my people. Let me use my gift to do something for them.

Tomorrow, I will discuss with Dr. Strauss the manner in which I can work in this area. I may be able to help him work out the problems of widespread use of the technique which was used on me. I have several good ideas of my own.

There is so much that might be done with this technique. If I could be made into a genius, what about thousands of others like myself? What fantastic levels might be achieved by using this technique on normal people? On geniuses?

There are so many doors to open. I am impatient to begin.

PROGRESS REPORT 13

May 23   It happened today. Algernon bit me. I visited the lab to see him as I do occasionally, and when I took him out of his cage, he snapped at my hand. I put him back and watched him for a while. He was unusually disturbed and vicious.

May 24   Burt, who is in charge of the experimental animals, tells me that Algernon is changing. He is less co-operative; he refuses to run the maze any more; general motivation has decreased. And he hasn't been eating. Everyone is upset about what this may mean.

May 25   They've been feeding Algernon, who now refuses to work the shifting-lock problem. Everyone identifies me with Algernon. In a way we're the first of our kind. They're all pretending that Algernon's behavior is not necessarily significant for me.

But it's hard to hide the fact that some of the other animals who were used in this experiment are showing strange behavior.

Dr. Strauss and Dr. Nemur have asked me not to come to the lab any more. I know what they're thinking but I can't accept it. I am going ahead with my plans to carry their research forward. With all due respect to both of these fine scientists, I am well aware of their limitations. If there is an answer, I'll have to find it out for myself. Suddenly, time has become very important to me.

May 29   I have been given a lab of my own and permission to go ahead with the research. I'm on to something. Working day and night. I've had a cot moved into the lab. Most of my writing time is spent on the notes which I keep in a separate folder, but from time to time I feel it necessary to put down my moods and my thoughts out of sheer habit.

I find the *calculus of intelligence* to be a fascinating study. Here is the place for the application of all the knowledge I have acquired. In a sense it's the problem I've been concerned with all my life.

May 31   Dr. Strauss thinks I'm working too hard. Dr. Nemur says I'm trying to cram a lifetime of research and thought into a few weeks. I know I should rest, but I'm driven on by something inside that won't let me stop. I've got to find the reason for the sharp regression in Algernon. I've got to know if and when it will happen to me.

June 4
LETTER TO DR. STRAUSS (copy)
Dear Dr. Strauss:
    Under separate cover I am sending you a copy of my report entitled, "The Algernon-Gordon Effect: A Study of Structure and Function of Increased Intelligence," which I would like to have you read and have published.

As you see, my experiments are completed. I have included in my report all of my formulae, as well as mathematical analysis in the appendix. Of course, these should be verified.

Because of its importance to both you and Dr. Nemur (and need I say to myself, too?) I have checked and rechecked my results a dozen times in the hope of finding an error. I am sorry to say the results must stand. Yet for the sake of science, I am grateful for the little bit that I here add to the knowledge of the function of the human mind and of the laws governing the artificial increase of human intelligence.

I recall your once saying to me that an experimental *failure* or the *disproving* of a theory was as important to the advancement of learning as a success would be. I know now that this is true. I am sorry, however, that my own contribution to the field must rest upon the ashes of the work of two men I regard so highly.

Yours truly,
Charles Gordon

encl.:rept.

June 5   I must not become emotional. The facts and the results of my experiments are clear, and the more sensational aspects of my own rapid climb cannot obscure the fact that the tripling of intelligence by the surgical technique developed by Drs. Strauss and Nemur must be viewed as having little or no practical applicability (at the present time) to the increase of human intelligence.

As I review the records and data on Algernon, I see that although he is still in his physical infancy, he has regressed mentally. Motor activity is impaired; there is a general reduction of glandular activity; there is an accelerated loss of co-ordination. There are also strong indications of progressive amnesia.

As will be seen by my report, these and other physical and mental deterioration syndromes can be predicted with statistically significant results by the application of my formula.

The surgical stimulus to which we were both subjected has resulted in an intensification and acceleration of all mental processes. The unforeseen development, which I have taken the liberty of calling the *Algernon-Gordon Effect,* is the logical extension of the entire intelligence speed-up. The hypothesis here proven may be described simply in the following terms: Artificially increased intelligence deteriorates at a rate of time directly proportional to the quantity of the increase.

I feel that this, in itself, is an important discovery.

As long as I am able to write, I will continue to record my thoughts in these progress reports. It is one of my few pleasures. However, by all indications, my own mental deterioration will be very rapid.

I have already begun to notice signs of emotional instability and forgetfulness, the first symptoms of burnout.

June 10   Deterioration progressing. I have become absent-minded. Algernon died two days ago. Dissection shows my predictions were right. His brain has decreased in weight.

I guess the same thing is or will soon be happening to me. Now that it's definite, I don't want it to happen. I put Algernon's body in a cheese box and buried him in the back yard. I cried.

June 15   Dr. Strauss came to see me again. I wouldn't open the door and I told him to go away. I want to be left to myself. I have become touchy and irritable. I feel the darkness closing in. It's hard to throw off thoughts of suicide. I keep telling myself how important this introspective journal will be.

It's a strange sensation to pick up a book that you've read and enjoyed just a few months ago and discover that you don't remember it. I remembered how great I thought John Milton was, but when I picked up *Paradise Lost* I couldn't understand it at all. I got so angry I threw the book across the room.

I've got to try to hold on to some of it. Some of the things I've learned. Oh, God, please don't take it all away.

June 19 Sometimes, at night, I go out for a walk. Last night I couldn't remember where I lived. A policeman took me home. I have the strange feeling that this has all happened to me before—a long time ago. I keep telling myself I'm the only person in the world who can describe what's happening to me.

June 21 Why can't I remember? I've got to fight. I lie in bed for days and I don't know who or where I am. Then it all comes back to me in a flash. Fugues of amnesia. Symptoms of senility—second childhood. I can watch them coming on. It's so cruelly logical. I learned so much and so fast. Now my mind is deteriorating rapidly. I won't let it happen. I'll fight it. I can't help thinking of the boy in the restaurant, the blank expression, the silly smile, the people laughing at him. No—please—not that again . . .

June 22 I'm forgetting things that I learned recently. It seems to be following the classic pattern—the last things learned are the first things forgotten. Or is that the pattern? I'd better look it up again. . . .

I reread my paper on the *Algernon-Gordon Effect* and I get the strange feeling that it was written by someone else. There are parts I don't even understand.

Motor activity impaired. I keep tripping over things, and it becomes increasingly difficult to type.

June 23 I've given up using the typewriter completely. My co-ordination is bad. I feel that I'm moving slower and slower. Had a terrible shock today. I picked up a copy of an article I used in my research, Krueger's *Uber Psychische Ganzheit*, to see if it would help me understand what I had done. First I thought there was something wrong with my eyes. Then I realized I could no longer read German. I tested myself in other languages. All gone.

June 30 A week since I dared to write again. It's slipping away like sand through my fingers. Most of the books I have are too hard for me now. I get angry with them because I know that I read and understood them just a few weeks ago.

I keep telling myself I must keep writing these reports so that somebody will know what is happening to me. But it gets harder to form the words and remember spellings. I have to look up even simple words in the dictionary now and it makes me impatient with myself.

Dr. Strauss comes around almost every day, but I told him I wouldn't see or speak to anybody. He feels guilty. They all do. But I don't blame anyone. I knew what might happen. But how it hurts.

July 7 I don't know where the week went. Today's Sunday I know because I can see through my window people going to church. I think I stayed in bed all week but I remember Mrs. Flynn bringing food to me a few times. I keep saying over and over ive got to do something but then I forget or maybe its just easier not to do what I say Im going to do.

I think of my mother and father a lot these days. I found a picture of them with me taken at a beach. My father has a big ball under his arm and my mother is holding me by the hand. I dont remember them the way they are in the picture. All I remember is my father drunk most of the time and arguing with mom about money.

He never shaved much and he used to scratch my face when he hugged me. My mother said he died but Cousin Miltie said he heard his mom and dad say that my father ran away with another woman. When I asked my mother she slapped my face and said my father was dead. I dont think I ever found out which was true but I don't care much. (He said he was going to take me to see cows on a farm once but he never did. He never kept his promises...)

July 10   My landlady Mrs Flynn is very worried about me. She says the way I lay around all day and dont do anything I remind her of her son before she threw him out of the house. She said she doesnt like loafers. If Im sick its one thing, but if Im a loafer thats another thing and she wont have it. I told her I think Im sick.

I try to read a little bit every day, mostly stories, but sometimes I have to read the same thing over and over again because I dont know what it means. And its hard to write. I know I should look up all the words in the dictionary but its so hard and Im so tired all the time.

Then I got the idea that I would only use the easy words instead of the long hard ones. That saves time. I put flowers on Algernons grave about once a week. Mrs Flynn thinks Im crazy to put flowers on a mouses grave but I told her that Algernon was special.

July 14   Its sunday again. I dont have anything to do to keep me busy now because my television set is broke and I dont have any money to get it fixed. (I think I lost this months check from the lab. I dont remember)

I get awful headaches and asperin doesnt help me much. Mrs Flynn knows Im really sick and she feels very sorry for me. Shes a wonderful woman whenever someone is sick.

July 22 Mrs Flynn called a strange doctor to see me. She was afraid I was going to die. I told the doctor I wasnt too sick and that I only forget sometimes. He asked me did I have any friends or relatives and I said no I dont have any. I told him I had a friend called Algernon once but he was a mouse and we used to run races together. He looked at me kind of funny like he thought I was crazy.

He smiled when I told him I used to be a genius. He talked to me like I was a baby and he winked at Mrs Flynn. I got mad and chased him out because he was making fun of me the way they all used to.

July 24 I have no more money and Mrs Flynn says I got to go to work somewhere and pay the rent because I havent paid for over two months. I dont know any work but the job I used to have at Donnegans Plastic Box Company I dont want to go back there because they all knew me when I was smart and maybe theyll laugh at me. But I dont know what else to do to get money.

July 25 I was looking at some of my old progress reports and its very funny but I cant read what I wrote. I can make out some of the words but they dont make sense.

Miss Kinnian came to the door but I said go away I dont want to see you. She cried and I cried too but I wouldnt let her in because I didnt want her to laugh at me. I told her I didn't like her any more. I told her I didnt want to be smart any more. Thats not true. I still love her and I still want to be smart but I had to say that so shed go away. She gave Mrs Flynn money to pay the rent. I dont want that. I got to get a job.

Please...please let me not forget how to read and write...

July 27   Mr Donnegan was very nice when I came back and asked him for my old job of janitor. First he was very suspicious but I told him what happened to me then he looked very sad and put his hand on my shoulder and said Charlie Gordon you got guts.

Everybody looked at me when I came downstairs and started working in the toilet sweeping it out like I used to. I told myself Charlie if they make fun of you dont get sore because you remember their not so smart as you once thot they were. And besides they were once your friends and if they laughed at you that doesnt mean anything because they liked you too.

One of the new men who came to work there after I went away made a nasty crack he said hey Charlie I hear your a very smart fella a real quiz kid. Say something intelligent. I felt bad but Joe Carp came over and grabbed him by the shirt and said leave him alone you lousy cracker or Ill break your neck. I didnt expect Joe to take my part so I guess hes really my friend.

Later Frank Reilly came over and said Charlie if anybody bothers you or trys to take advantage you call me or Joe and we will set em straight. I said thanks Frank and I got choked up so I had to turn around and go into the supply room so he wouldnt see me cry. Its good to have friends.

July 28   I did a dumb thing today I forgot I wasnt in Miss Kinnians class at the adult center any more like I use to be. I went in and sat down in my old seat in the back of the room and she looked at me funny and she said Charles. I dint remember she ever called me that before only Charlie so I said hello Miss Kinnian Im redy for my lesin today only I lost my reader that we was using. She startid to cry and run out of the room and everybody looked at me and I saw they wasnt the same pepul who used to be in my class.

Then all of a suddin I rememberd some things about the operashun and me getting smart and I said holy smoke I reely pulled a Charlie Gordon that time. I went away before she come back to the room.

Thats why Im going away from New York for good. I dont want to do nothing like that agen. I dont want Miss Kinnian to feel sorry for me. Evry body feels sorry at the factery and I dont want that eather so Im going someplace where nobody knows that Charlie Gordon was once a genus and now he cant even reed a book or rite good.

Im taking a cuple of books along and even if I cant reed them Ill practise hard and maybe I wont forget every thing I lerned. If I try reel hard maybe Ill be a littel bit smarter then I was before the operashun. I got my rabits foot and my luky penny and maybe they will help me.

If you ever reed this Miss Kinnian dont be sorry for me Im glad I got a second chanse to be smart becaus I lerned a lot of things that I never even new were in this world and Im grateful that I saw it all for a littel bit. I dont know why Im dumb agen or what I did wrong maybe its becaus I dint try hard enuff. But if I try and practis very hard maybe Ill get a littl smarter and know what all the words are. I remember a littel bit how nice I had a feeling with the blue book that has the torn cover when I red it. Thats why Im gonna keep trying to get smart so I can have that feeling agen. Its a good feeling to know things and be smart. I wish I had it rite now if I did I would sit down and reed all the time. Anyway I bet Im the first dumb person in the world who ever found out somthing importent for sience. I remember I did somthing but I dont remember what. So I gess its like I did it for all the dumb pepul like me.

Good-by Miss Kinnian and Dr Strauss and evreybody.

And P.S. please tell Dr Nemur not to be such a grouch when pepul laff at him and he woud have more frends. Its easy to make frends if you let pepul laff at you. Im going to have lots of frends where I go.

P.P.S. Please if you get a chanse put some flowrs on Algernons grave in the bak yard...